COLLECTOR'S ENCYCLOPEDIA OF

Red Wing
ART POTTERY

IDENTIFICATION & VALUES

B. L. & R. L.
DOLLEN

COLLECTOR BOOKS
A Division of Schroeder Publishing Co., Inc.

FRONT COVER, clockwise from top:
  Bob White dinner plate, 11", bottom marked, turquoise/brown, $22.00 – 32.00 each.
  Vase #1196 — 10", gloss gray/yellow, purple/flower handle vase, $48.00 – 62.00.
  Vase #1174 — 7", semi-matte pink/ivory, leaf embossed, $48.00 – 62.00.
  Plain pattern salt & pepper, 3", no bottom mark, turquoise/pink, $22.00 – 30.00 set.
  Miniature pitcher, 4", bottom marked, turquoise, $55.00 – 70.00.
  Friar Tuck cookie jar, bottom marked, yellow/brown, $110.00 – 140.00.

BACK COVER:
  Top — Vase #763 — 8", gloss bronze/Tahitian gold, urn style, $56.00 – 70.00.
  Bottom right — Plain pattern creamer, 2", bottom marked, turquoise, $14.00 – 20.00.
  Bottom left — Magnolia candleholders, #1228 — 4½", ivory/brown wipe, $22.00 – 30.00 each.

Cover Design: Beth Summers

Book Design: Ben Faust

Searching for a Publisher?

COLLECTOR BOOKS
P.O. Box 3009
Paducah, KY 42002-3009

www.collectorbooks.com

Contents

Dedication

Art pottery by definition is any article created by a gifted artist for beauty rather than utility and can encompass even tableware.

This book is dedicated to all the people who are Red Wing collectors, and to those who will join us in the future. It is a passion that, as we know, gives us great joy. It is the thrill of the hunt ... the joy of the find.

Acknowledgments

I wish to express my appreciation for the help I received in researching Red Wing art pottery at the Goodhue County Historical Society Library, located in Red Wing, Minnesota. Also, thanks for assistance at the research center of the Minnesota Historical Society, located in St. Paul, Minnesota.

Everyone connected with research at these two institutions was very helpful in their assistance.

Reference materials used at the Goodhue County Historical Society were copies of original Red Wing catalogs dated 1930s through 1965, held by the Goodhue County Historical Society.

Reference materials used at the Minnesota Historical Society were original Red Wing catalogs dated 1956 through 1966, held in the archives of the Minnesota Historical Society.

Special Acknowledgment

I would like to give a special thank you to Bev and Duane Brown who own and operate B & D Collectibles & Antiques in Harlan, Iowa. Allowing me to photograph pieces from their collection contributed significantly to this book.

Also, thanks to my husband Roger, for driving me many miles in search of information for this book.

Photographs by Troy A. Petry

Pricing and Value Guide

The prices included in this book are not meant to set prices. They are a general guide on the pricing which can vary considerably due to demand and the area where the item is purchased. The price ranges in this book are an average of prices from different areas of the country. The pricing given assumes that the pottery is in very good condition. Cracks or chips take away from a piece's value. In turn, pieces in perfect condition command higher prices.

You may find some bargain prices at yard sales, auctions, and thrift stores. However, people at thrift stores and auctions are now more knowledgeable about antiques, and you will find most of them separate the antiques and sell them at considerably higher prices than the other items.

You will also find some areas of the country where the prices are considerably higher which result from several factors. As a general guide for pricing, you will find those in this book to be in the range of most available Red Wing art pottery.

About This Book

This book is an identification and value guide, intended to help you identify a piece of Red Wing Art Pottery and give an average price you can expect to pay for the item. As stated above, these prices will vary.

Pieces of Red Wing art pottery are considered antiques. You will need to look in antique stores to find them, individual stores or antique malls which have a number of dealers selling items.

Red Wing may also be available at some auctions and antiques sales. There may be occasions that you are lucky enough to find some pieces at yard sales, but to find any quantity or selection you will probably have to stay with antique locales. There are several monthly antique papers that carry a listing of sales and auctions. Some of the art pottery is also available at larger antique stores and malls.

You may look in several stores or go to several sales to find any Red Wing. Some auctions may have whole collections of Red Wing for sale. The larger auctions usually list what antiques will be available, so you will know before you attend.

Now that you have an idea of where to look, you can read this book and pick out a piece you like. You will know the approximate price you will have to pay and you can start looking for Red Wing art pottery.

Happy hunting …

Introduction

Red Wing fever … it has taken the country by surprise. When the Art Pottery Line was originally introduced by Red Wing in the early 1930s, it offered a way for the company to both diversify and give consumers a line of vases and other items to use in their homes. Today it is one of the most sought after collectibles in the art pottery field. For years, many people enjoyed collecting the Stoneware Line of Red Wing, and as they collected, the values grew. Now art pottery has come into its own and is finding a place in the history of collectibles.

The fever started for me with one planter left to me by my late mother. It was matte white with a green interior and fancy flower handles. You could tell by looking at it that it was a quality item of that era. I loved that planter, not only because it belonged to my mother, but also because it looked great anywhere I put it. I had determined by this time that it was Red Wing.

I had the planter for several years, when one day while looking in an antique store, I saw a vase that caught my eye. It was the same colors and style as my favorite Red Wing. In checking, I found it indeed was Red Wing, so I purchased the vase to go with the planter I had. Well, it was not long before I was looking for Red Wing everywhere we went and purchasing my finds. Suddenly I knew I was hooked … and so my collection grew.

While I was collecting, I looked for a book to help guide me in my purchases, but I could not find a book on the art pottery. I decided to do some research and write a book on Red Wing art pottery on the values, age, and perhaps names of some of the lines of art ware, not only for myself, but also to help others who, like me, get a great deal of pleasure from collecting Red Wing. From what I understand, there are a great number of us in the United States who have Red Wing fever.

If you have ever looked for Red Wing art pottery, you have no doubt noticed there were many different pieces and colors of pottery produced by Red Wing. This book does not contain every piece of pottery produced but will give you a broad scope of the many different pieces you can look for and find.

There is something about articles from the past that create a certain ambiance wherever they are placed. They have a certain style that is never outdated; it is only enhanced by time. Their value also increases with age, as people learn to appreciate their quality and style.

If you have a collection, check out your pieces. If you do not have any Red Wing, hopefully reading this book will get you excited enough to go out and look for some. Look around and find a piece you like, purchase it, and check the book to see if you have found a rare item or perhaps a bargain. Whatever you get will be sure to add beauty and style to any setting. The possibilities of what you can find are endless, as is the joy you will get from collecting

Chances are good, that you too can catch Red Wing fever … enjoy.

History of Red Wing

In 1861 a German immigrant, Joseph Pohl, settled on a farm near Red Wing, Minnesota. He soon discovered that the clays near the farm were excellent for making utilitarian wares such as crocks and churns. He started making these stoneware items in an old schoolhouse and sold them to the local citizens. Pohl left the area around the time of the Civil War, but he is credited with discovering the clay around Red Wing.

In 1868 David Hallem began operating a stoneware pottery in his home in Red Wing. This venture was not successful and was eventually purchased by a group of citizens who formed a corporation under the name of Red Wing Stoneware Company. Hallem was the first to supervise this operation in 1878. The venture proved successful, and Red Wing Stoneware Company was recognized as one of the leading producers of stoneware in the United States.

Soon two competitors entered the field, Minnesota Stoneware Company in 1883, and Northstar in 1892. After four years the Northstar Company closed. In the early 1900s both Red Wing Stoneware Company and Minnesota Stoneware Company burned. After each constructed a new plant, the two companies merged forming Red Wing Union Stoneware Company.

They later introduced a pottery line in addition to the stoneware line. Eventually the company created an art ware line. The Brushed Ware Line was the first decorative art ware introduced in the late 1920s. In 1930 they introduced the Glazed Ware art pottery lines with fine smooth glazes and classical shapes.

The name of the pottery was changed in 1936 from Red Wing Union Stoneware Company to Red Wing Potteries Inc. Sometime in the early 1930s, Red Wing contracted to produce a line of art pottery for a marketing agent in Little Rock, Arkansas, named George Rumrill. Rumrill designed a lot of the items in this line which was named after him, RumRill. Red Wing continued to produce the line until 1938 when Rumrill ceased purchasing from Red Wing, and contracted other eastern potteries to produce his wares.

Red Wing discontinued the stoneware line in 1947 and continued to produce the art pottery lines until 1967 when labor problems and a dwindling market forced them to close their doors. Red Wing potteries had been producing their wares for 89 years at the time they closed.

The remaining stock was sold piece by piece at a salesroom across the street from the pottery. A legend in their field, Red Wing Potteries will never be forgotten.

RED WING HISTORY CHART

1878	Red Wing Union Stoneware Company
1883	Minnesota Stoneware Company (competitor)
1892	Northstar Company (competitor)
1896	Northstar Company out of business
1900	Minnesota Stoneware Co. burns (spring)
1900	Red Wing Union Stoneware burns (fall)

(Both companies rebuild and merge)

1908	Red Wing Union Stoneware Company (official reincorporating) (Trademark RED WING)
1929	Introduced Art Ware Line
1930	Introduced Fine Art Pottery Line
1935	Introduced Dinnerware Line
1936	Red Wing Potteries (legal name change)
1947	Ceased production of stoneware
1967	Plant closed

Learning About & Collecting Red Wing Art Pottery

Learning About Red Wing Art Pottery

The Art Pottery Line of Red Wing was first introduced in the 1920s with the Brushwork Line. The pottery was a crude line using the same clay they used to make the Stoneware Line, with some modifications.

In the late 1930s, due to a decrease in the market for the Stoneware Line and because the local clay supply was running out, they hired Belle Koran, a New York designer, to design a line of fine art pottery. Art pottery by definition is any article created by a gifted artist, for beauty rather than utility, and could encompass even tableware. This line required blended earthen clays, which the producers imported from other states. The pottery had fine smooth glazes and classical forms. The lines were very ornate, each having distinctive handles and base decorations that matched their names. A list and description of the lines follow this chapter. The first lines produced by Red Wing and RumRill are very hard to find.

The glazes on the art ware were soft velvety matte, semi-matte, and gloss in an array of colors. One of the most popular lines is the soft ivory matte with purplish brown sprayed on and wiped off, leaving color in the recesses. Belle Kogan created these lines, among them the Renaissance, Magnolia, and Vintage Lines. This method of using color is seen on raised designs of fruits and flowers on vases, bowls, and other items.

Ivory With Brown Wipe Method. These pieces are an example of the ivory with brown wipe lines. Note the dark coloring in the recesses.

They later simplified the early lines and standardized them, producing these lines throughout the 1950s and 1960s. Eva Zeisel, another New York designer, created other art ware and the Town and Country Dinnerware Line introduced in 1946.

Glazes

One of the most attractive aspects of the art ware was the use of different color glazes to decorate a single article. One shade was used on the outside, and a different color lined the inside, such as white with green, pink with white, blue with pink, and others.

Multicolored and Plain Glazes. These pieces are examples of the color glazes. The multicolored glazes came in many different two-tone colors. The plain colors were more limited.

Types of Glaze Finish. These pieces show the different type of glazes used over the years. There was matte, shown on the green mandarin bowl, semi matte, shown on the white and green snifter vase, and gloss, shown on the yellow and brown snail shaped vase.

Bottom Markings

All the art ware made by Red Wing was numbered and marked "Red Wing" on the bottom of each piece. The marks were of several varieties, but all had Red Wing in them. The earlier Brushware Line had an ink stamp marking. One stamp was a circle with the wording Red Wing Union Stoneware, Red Wing Minn. Another stamp had Red Wing Art Pottery with no circle. The bottom markings on the later art ware were inscribed by hand.

Following are a few of the bottom markings. Note the numbers on the later art ware.

Brushware. The bottom marking on a Brushware vase. Notice that there are no numbers.

RumRill. The bottom marking on a RumRill bowl. The numbering system on RumRill was done starting with lower numbers.

Red Wing 1940s. The bottom markings on a 1940s vintage Red Wing vase.

Red Wing Pitcher. The bottom marking on a small Red Wing pitcher. Notice the lack of numbers. The pitcher was probably part of the Dinnerware Line which was not numbered.

RumRill

One exception to the Red Wing markings was the late 1930s Red Wing contract to produce a line of art ware for George Rumrill. All of the art ware produced for him was marked "RumRill" on the bottom. RumRill pieces were also numbered. George Rumrill created many of his own designs, but some of his articles were made from the Red Wing molds.

You can find some pieces of Red Wing and RumRill that are identical except for the bottom markings. George Rumrill ceased purchasing his wares from Red Wing in 1938.

RumRill. This group shows a few pieces of the RumRill line. Note the similar color glaze style in the two-tone colors that Red Wing used.

Wing Labels

Some Red Wing art ware also had a paper wing label. The selection method for adding a paper label is not known, but articles that are found with the label intact are worth up to $10.00 more in value, depending on the item and the condition of the label. The wing labels came in gold or silver with a red wing and red lettering. There was also a smaller label with a different wing shape, red with silver markings. Some special edition labels have also been found. One such label is gold with a red wing and the inscription, "75th Year, Red Wing, 1878 – 1953."

Silver Wing Label. An example of the silver wing label. Notice that it reads "Red Wing Art Pottery."

Gold Wing Label. A gold label with markings identical to the silver label. The only difference is the gold color. The labels were placed randomly on the pieces of pottery; some were even placed sideways.

Anniversary Wing Label. One of the special wing labels done in gold and red. Notice the writing denoting their 75th Anniversary.

Red Wing Label. An example of the different red label. This was probably the original label used in the 1930s and later changed to the bigger silver and gold label. You do not find many pieces with this label.

Shape Numbers

Red Wing produced a catalog of their wares for wholesale and retail business. The early catalogs were numbered on the front. In the 1950s and 1960s they had Spring and Fall catalogs marked on the front of the catalog. The number markings on the bottom of the art ware were the production and catalog numbers of that particular item. The numbers began with the first lines of art pottery in the 1930s and 1940s, starting with the 100 series. This number stayed with the piece throughout the production of that particular piece. Some of the pieces were produced from the beginning in the 1930s on through the 1960s. In the 1950s and 1960s the numbering system went up through the 5000 series. At no time, however, did Red Wing use all the numbers in a given series. Some of the numbers have a letter preceding them, such as B1409. Belle Kogan put a B in front of the numbers on some of the articles she designed. Designer Charles Murphy added the initial M in front of some numbers.

Red Wing also might add or drop a color from a line from the Spring to Fall catalog. In doing so, they may have been limiting the number of a certain colored piece. All colors were not always available. The art ware was sold differently at given times. An item may have been available to purchase by individual piece in one catalog and by the dozen in another.

The following pieces show examples of some of the different numbers that are found on the bottom of Red Wing art ware.

Plain Numbers. These pieces show examples of how only numbers were used on some items.

Letter and Number. These pieces show examples of a designer adding his or her initial before the number. The M is for Charles Murphy and there would be a B for Belle Kogan on her pieces. Also notice the different positions for Red Wing USA in the bottom markings.

It is relatively easy to recognize a piece of Red Wing on sight, once you are familiar with the semi matte, two-tone coloring, or some of the other gloss colors. You can further identify the piece by looking at the bottom markings.

Art Pottery 1930s – 1960s

These pieces give an overall view of some of the Red Wing art ware you can find.

Art Pottery 1930 – 1960. These pieces range from the first art pottery of the 1930s through the 1960s. Notice the array of colors used in the later pieces. Clockwise from top: 1950s, 1940s, 1960s, and 1930s.

Collecting Red Wing Art Pottery

There are a variety of reasons why and how people collect Red Wing art pottery. I am sure there is a category you will fit into among them.

Some collect a few pieces that simply caught their eye. These collectors use the items in their homes. They put flowers in the vases, display fruit or other things in the bowls, and use the candleholders with candles that match their decor. Their collection is used strictly for personal enjoyment.

The next category is the serious collector, who purchases many pieces of Red Wing art pottery and owns a large collection, which can consist of several hundred pieces. Serious collectors are usually looking at their collection as an investment. They have collected for many years, and therefore have purchased a lot of the pieces at prices that are lower than today's value. As Red Wing art pottery increases in popularity, the future prices can be higher than they are today. Red Wing art pottery is fast becoming one of the hot collectibles in today's market. Therefore, a collection can increase in value over time and can be worth considerably more than the purchase price, making it not only a good investment, but also giving you some quality pieces to display in the home.

Still another category are the collectors somewhere in between who purchase Red Wing pottery for resale. They are constantly buying and selling their items. Often they rent a booth in one of the many antique malls throughout the United States and make a profit selling their Red Wing purchases.

How people collect is often done according to the reason they are collecting. The serious collector usually purchases any Red Wing art ware they do not have in their collection, and some even purchase duplicate pieces. The resale collector will purchase any art ware they find that is priced within their price range that would allow for a mark-up at the time of sale. Those collecting to display often purchase the art ware that catches their eye or is a color they want for their decor.

As-Is Art Pottery

Whatever your reason for collecting, there is one thing you will need to remember. Any damage, such as cracks or chips on an item, reduces the value of the piece considerably no matter how small. You will find that you can get some bargain prices on art pottery sold as-is.

Most damaged pottery will be marked as such, but you will need to examine the piece even if it is not marked as-is in case the seller overlooked the damage.

If you are collecting simply to display the art pottery in your home, condition will not be as big a factor to you, and by purchasing damaged pieces you will not have to make as large an investment. However, if you are purchasing as an investment or for resale, any damage can greatly reduce your profit.

Ways to Organize a Collection

There are numerous ways a collection can be organized. A few of these are by **item**, **color**, **specific line**, **novelty pieces**, and **miniatures** or for display. Here are some ideas in each of these categories.

Collecting by **item** can be done in several different ways. You can have a whole collection consisting of different pieces of one item such as vases. This could also be done with any of the art pottery such as bowls, planters or candleholders. Arranging a collection of one item in different colors also works out very well. Red Wing produced many shapes that were each finished in a wide array of colors. A couple of good examples for this collection would be vase #505 shown in the miscellaneous group of the RumRill section. This shape was also produced in the Red Wing line in a multitude of beautiful colors such as the one shown in the 1950s section. Another example is the fan vase #892 shown in the Floraline section of the 1960s art pottery. This vase also was produced in many lovely colors. Any of these would be a collection anyone would be proud to own and would provide a beautiful display.

Color is another very good way to organize your collection. This can be accomplished by purchasing different pieces of art pottery all with the same color finish. Since the colors in the finishes used by Red Wing were produced over and over, many of the colors would give a wide array of different items. A good example of this is the Luster Blue/Coral finish. You will find a vase #1160 in the 1940s section in this color. There are also more examples of this finish throughout the book. The fleck colors would also make a great collection. Vase #M1457 in the 1950s section shows an example of the fleck yellow finish. There is also fleck Nile blue, fleck zephyr pink, and fleck green, which you will see throughout the book. Other colors that would be good for this type of collection are white, black, blue, and a combination of black and white items.

A collection by **specific line** works very well. Magnolia is one very good example of this type of organization. You will see examples of Magnolia in the 1920s & 1930s section. There were also novelty pieces produced in Magnolia, such as a small box and a small ashtray, to provide diversity to a collection.

Brushed Ware would also make an excellent collection. Although not as colorful as the others, it would be a valuable collection since it was the first art pottery produced by Red Wing. Another valuable and also colorful collection would be Rum-Rill. These specific line collections are ones that any other collector would envy. However, you will find them to be more expensive than some of the other collections and also harder to find.

Novelty pieces also make a fun collection. Red Wing produced many different kinds of novelty planters, such as a deer, giraffe, donkey, swan, rabbit, owl, and dachshund. A collection of these items would be very novel. Again these items are harder to find and more expensive, but the resulting collection would be worthwhile.

If your display space is limited, collecting **miniatures** is a good way to handle that. Red Wing produced a number of miniature vases and planters. These are quite hard to find and also quite expensive, but the results are not only ornate but also very valuable.

Looking for specific items to purchase will take some time. But as we collectors know, the hunt is a large part of the fun. And when you complete a collection such as these examples, you will be very pleased.

Throughout the book you will find items noted for these collections. However, the possibilities are limited only to your imagination. Red Wing art pottery has a look of quality that enhances any setting in which it is placed. No matter how your collection is organized or what your reason is for collecting, you will be able to find many places in your home to display your Red Wing.

Art Pottery Displays

This section has several examples of ways to display Red Wing art pottery. You can be sure that anyone collecting is also displaying some of their art ware.

Many different pottery pieces can be displayed on a dining room table and will add charm to your home. Below is an example of this, with a display from the Magnolia Line of Red Wing.

Magnolia Line Display. Magnolia Vase, #1030 — 9", $70.00 – 90.00. Magnolia Candleholders, #1228 — 4½", $22.00 – 30.00 each. These pieces are all finished in the ivory/brown wipe method.

A piano display gives a very elegant look to your music room. Below the piano is displayed with a Red Wing violin planter along with a RumRill vase. Red Wing also made a banjo and a small piano in the music line planters.

Red Wing Violin Planter & RumRill Vase. Violin Wall Planter, #1484 — 13", semi-matte black, $48.00 – 58.00. Rum-Rill Vase #641 – 7", matte aqua/gloss white, $56.00 – 70.00.

A replica of an antique wash stand displays almost any piece of pottery exquisitely. Below we have a Red Wing Vintage Line pitcher vase and candleholders in lieu of a bowl and pitcher.

Vintage Line Pitcher Vase & Candleholders. Vintage Pitcher Vase, #616 — 11", semi-matte ivory/brown wipe, $145.00 – 225.00. Vintage Candleholders, #622 – 5½", semi-matte ivory/brown wipe, $48.00 – 64.00 pair.

Displayed on the buffet below is a Red Wing Deluxe Line console set. As you can see, this set adds color and warmth to the room and accents the picture in the background.

Red Wing Deluxe Line Console Set. Deluxe Line Ivy Bowl, #B2504 — 14½", gloss green, $85.00 – 110.00. Deluxe Line Swan Figurine, #B2506 — 9", gloss green, $95.00 – 125.00. Deluxe Line Ivy Candlesticks, B2505 – 4½", gloss green, $45.00 – 60.00 pair.

A grouping of vases on a marble top table adds the touch of color you need for any room. The table below displays Red Wing and RumRill vases.

Red Wing & RumRill Vases. Center front, clockwise, Red Wing miniature vase, #873 — 4½", semi-matte yellow, $55.00 – 68.00. RumRill Vase, #291 — 5½", semi-matte ocean green, $55.00 - 72.00. Red Wing Chromoline vase, #637 — 8", gloss blue/yellow combination, $85.00 – 98.00. RumRill vase, #500 — 5½", semi-matte Dutch blue/stipple, $75.00 – 90.00.

If you do not have an antique setting in your home, Red Wing looks just as elegant on any type of furniture. The smaller collections such as miniatures or novelty planters can be displayed on a shelf in a hutch, a hanging shelf on a wall, or on an occasional table. When collecting miniatures, you will find they are higher in price than some of the other art pottery since they are scarce.

Other collections of Red Wing you might consider are the dinnerware, cookie jars, or water coolers. The dinnerware was produced in many lovely patterns, some of which can be seen beginning on page 113. Dinnerware can be displayed in a hutch or around the top of the kitchen on a shelf. You can also set a beautiful table with an entire dinnerware set of the same pattern. The cookie jar or water cooler could be used as functional items in the kitchen.

Water Coolers

Red Wing water coolers were produced in many of the dinnerware patterns. A collection of coolers is quite an accomplishment since they are scarce and very expensive. It would, however, be very unique and quite valuable.

The water cooler at left shows that a pleasant touch is added to the kitchen where a cooler is used to dispense water.

Red Wing Water Cooler. Tampico 2-gallon water cooler with stand, $600.00 – 750.00. From the collection of Bev & Duane Brown.

Cookie Jars

Red Wing produced many types of cookie jars. Quite a number of them matched a dinnerware pattern. Others were shaped like fruit, and some were characters. There were Pierre the Chef, a girl called the Katrina, and the King of Tarts, among others. The King of Tarts is a much sought after piece. Prices can range up to $900.00 for this cookie jar, which looks like a court jester.

The cookie jar pictured below shows how these pieces add charm to a kitchen counter. The Red Wing cookie jars make a very interesting collection.

Red Wing Chef Cookie Jar. Bottom stamped "Red Wing Pottery Hand Painted," yellow with brown accents, $110.00 – 160.00 in very good condition. This cookie jar has two bottom markings; the other reads "Red Wing USA" inscribed under the glaze.

Whether you display your Red Wing in some of the ways suggested or in your own style, there is no doubt you can find Red Wing art pottery in a color or type suited to your decor.

The numerous pieces of Red Wing art pottery that were produced make it easy to find some that will fit your situation. With a little imagination, there is a collection suited to everyone. Use your imagination, along with this book, and go collect!

Art Pottery 1920s & 1930s

Brushed Ware

The Brushed Ware Line was the first art pottery produced by Red Wing. Introduced in the 1920s, it was made with the same clay used for the stoneware with some modifications. Brushed Ware was a rustic line, decorated with acorns, cranes, cattails, flowers, and leaves. Red Wing had been producing flowerpots in the same designs prior to the introduction of the art pottery vases.

George Hehr designed the first art pottery vases. Bowls, urns, jardinieres, and other vases, along with some specialty pieces, were later added to the line. All the pieces were a rustic design with a brushed color stain over a tan body. The colors of the stain were dark green, light green, bronze tan, and luster green. The inside of the pottery was covered in a luster glaze, usually the same color used on the outside.

While crude, Brushed Ware holds a special place in the history of the art pottery lines and in the hearts of collectors. It was the beginning of a pottery legend, the oldest line of Red Wing art pottery. Though not as refined as its later fine art pottery counterparts, it has a quality look that definitely fits the category of antique. A collection of Brushed Ware would be unique; you would own the items that were the beginning of an art pottery legend.

The art pottery in this book is from the author's collection, unless otherwise noted.

Vase. 7", bottom stamped "Red Wing Art Pottery." dark green, cattail design, $85.00 – 130.00. You could also purchase a tan stone flower-frog insert for these vases. Although rarely found with the insert, the value is higher, $125.00 – 150.00.

The rough look of this vase indicates that perhaps it was one of the first Brushed Ware items. Even the inside glaze is not as refined as some of the other Brushed Ware pieces.

Vase. 7", bottom stamped "Red Wing Art Pottery," bronze tan, swirl Brushed Ware vase, $65.00 – 90.00. The finish on this vase has sand-like texture.

Vase. 7", bottom stamped "Red Wing Union Stoneware Co.," dark green acorn design, Cleveland vase, $85.00 – 110.00.

A vase like this one, except with lion head handles and additional colors, was presented to Mrs. Grover Cleveland when she and the president visited Red Wing. The vase had her name and date inscribed around the rim. Copies of the vase with some variations were later mass-produced and were known as the Cleveland.

Vase. 10", bottom stamped, walnut green, cattail design, $110.00 – 150.00.

You can tell by looking at the Brushed Ware pieces that they were made from the same crude clay as the stoneware. The color was wiped on the outside of the clay, giving a tan and green or tan and blue look to the item. The color on the inside was done in a semi-matte glaze and often spilled over the edge of the pottery and was fired on there.

Vase. 8", bottom stamped, cobalt blue, cattail design, $90.00 – 110.00. The cobalt blue brushed ware is harder to find than the green and often has a higher price. This piece is from the collection of Bernice Ehlers, Shelby, IA.

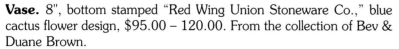

Vase. 8", bottom stamped "Red Wing Union Stoneware Co.," blue cactus flower design, $95.00 – 120.00. From the collection of Bev & Duane Brown.

Urn. 7", bottom stamped, walnut green, flower design, $90.00 – 120.00. Note the spill over of the green glaze used on the inside. This urn has a different bottom stamp; it reads "Red Wing Art Pottery."

Bowl. 6", bottom stamped, walnut green, Greek design, $65.00 – 90.00. The larger 10" bottom stamped, Greek design bowl is valued at $120.00 – 150.00.

Bowl. 9½", bottom stamped "Red Wing Art Pottery," dark green leaf design, bulb bowl, $95.00 – 135.00. These bowls were used to raise flowers indoors, such as tulips or daffodils. From the collection of Bev & Duane Brown.

Jardiniere. 9", bottom stamped, walnut green, leaf design, 10" diameter, $90.00 – 130.00.

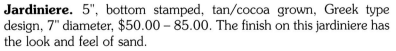

Jardiniere. 5", bottom stamped, tan/cocoa grown, Greek type design, 7" diameter, $50.00 – 85.00. The finish on this jardiniere has the look and feel of sand.

Pitcher. No bottom mark, dark green, rustic design, $150.00 – 185.00. There are mugs to match this pitcher (pictured below). With no handles they look more like glasses, but were known as mugs in the Red Wing catalog.

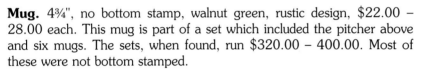

Mug. 4¾", no bottom stamp, walnut green, rustic design, $22.00 – 28.00 each. This mug is part of a set which included the pitcher above and six mugs. The sets, when found, run $320.00 – 400.00. Most of these were not bottom stamped.

Flower Pot with Bottom Saucer. 9", bottom stamped "Red Wing Union Stoneware Co.," dark green leaf design, 10" diameter. Saucer, 10" diameter, also bottom stamped. Set $140.00 – 175.00. This flowerpot was also sold without the saucer. Flowerpots alone, $95.00 – 135.00. These were made for greenhouse use and were the first items produced after the stoneware sales dwindled in 1922.

Glazed Ware

Glazed Ware was the next art pottery introduced by Red Wing. Vases were the first items produced; they were plain Egyptian style art ware, produced in a semi-matte glaze of clear bright greens, yellows, blues, and maroons. There were also combinations of white and colors. Later the Glazed Ware included various shaped vases, bowls, urns, planters, candlesticks, and some novelty items. The colors included the ones listed above and other combination colors. A list of some of the early Glazed Ware colors is on page 149.

Quite scarce, these early Glazed Ware pieces command high prices because they are some of the oldest Red Wing art pottery and are difficult to find. You will also notice that in spite of being the first glazed art ware produced by Red Wing using unrefined techniques, the pieces are quite beautiful. They have the look of something produced in a later era.

Red Wing continued to sell the Brushed Ware line along with the glazed art ware, giving each separate pages and price lists in the catalogs. Most of the Brushed Ware was bottom stamped only. The early Glaze Ware was bottom stamped with the same marking but was also engraved with a shape number. Examples of these marks are in the bottom marking section beginning on page 145.

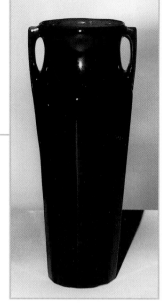

Vase. #154 — 12", bottom stamped, "Red Wing Art Pottery Co.," dark blue, Egyptian vase, $145.00 – 165.00. This blue is so dark that it looks almost black except in
very good light. Advertised in the Red Wing price list as dark blue or blue black, this
color commands higher prices than the other colors. This vase in maroon carries an
even higher price. From the collection of Bev & Duane Brown.

Vase. #154 — 12", bottom stamped "Red Wing Art Pottery," semi-matte light green,
Egyptian vase, $110.00 – 135.00. From the collection of Bev & Duane Brown.

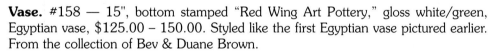

Vase. #158 — 15", bottom stamped "Red Wing Art Pottery," gloss white/green,
Egyptian vase, $125.00 – 150.00. Styled like the first Egyptian vase pictured earlier.
From the collection of Bev & Duane Brown.

Vase. #158 — 12", bottom stamped "Red Wing Art Pottery," gloss white/green, Egyptian vase, $110.00 – 135.00. From the collection of Bev & Duane Brown.

Vase. #157 — 12", bottom stamped "Red Wing Art Pottery," gloss green/white, Egyptian vase, $110.00 – 135.00. This is the same style vase as the previous ones, done in a different pattern and with the colors reversed.

Jugs. 8¾", bottom stamped "Red Wing Art Pottery," gloss blue, genie type jugs, $225.00 – 260.00 each. Some of the first Glazed Ware pottery, the jug came with a stopper in the same glaze and color as the jug. With stopper, $250.00 – 300.00. Perhaps used to water flowers or as cruets, these jugs are quite beautiful. From the collection of Bev & Duane Brown.

Fine Art Pottery Lines

The fine art pottery of Red Wing, which is also glazed ware, was produced starting in the 1930s. Due to a decrease in the market for the Stoneware line and because they were running out of the local clay they used, Red Wing hired designers Belle Kogan, Charles Murphy, and Eva Zeisel. They designed much of the early fine art pottery, which was made with blended earthen clays imported from other states. The pottery had fine smooth glazes and classical forms.

Some of the first lines, such as the nudes, are very hard to find and command high prices. The value of these early lines is hard to determine because they are not often found for sale. It is known that some of these early pieces of art ware have sold for prices up to $1,500. The prices of all the early 1920s and 1930s art pottery are rapidly increasing due to the age of the pottery and the availability.

The items produced were vases, bowls, compotes, candlesticks, planters, and jardinieres, along with some specialty items. The glazes on the art ware were soft velvety matte, semi-matte, and gloss in an array of colors.

Vase. #631 — 7½", semi-matte white/green, Greek style vase, $48.00 – 62.00.

Vase. #447 — 8", gloss coral/tan, sylvan style vase, $65.00 – 80.00. This vase is designed exactly like its Sylvan Line RumRill counterpart.

Vase. #1165 — 8¾", semi-matte ivory brown wipe, double handled, embossed vase, $62.00 – 75.00. From the collection of Bev & Duane Brown.

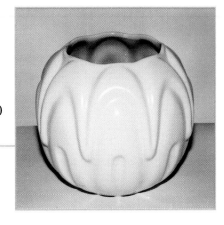

Vase. #1245 — 5½", semi-matte white/green, round vase, $48.00 – 62.00.

Medallion Line

The following pieces of art ware are from the Medallion Line produced in the late 1930s. The line consisted of several groups. These groups were produced in a semi-matte finish with a colored wipe on the recesses of the decorations which were flowers, grapes, and leaves. Some of the flower groups were called English Garden, Magnolia, and Cherry Blossom. The grape embossed pieces were called Vintage Group. The pieces embossed with leaves were called the Renaissance Group. The colors known are ivory, turquoise, yellow, and green and were finished with a brown wipe. There are also pieces glazed in ivory with a color wipe such as green or yellow. These wipe colors are very hard to find. The Medallion Line was one of the most popular art pottery lines Red Wing produced. Any of these groups would make a wonderful specific line collection.

English Garden Group

The English Garden Group, part of the Medallion Line, consisted of vases, bowls, and candleholders. As with the rest of the Medallion Line this group is known to have been produced in the ivory, turquoise, and yellow glazes, using brown, turquoise, or yellow wipe, in a semi-matte glaze. The pieces had unique ornate shapes and were very attractive. In any color, the English Garden pieces are quite hard to find.

Vase. #1187 — 12½", ivory/brown wipe, pitcher vase, $85.00 – 110.00. Notice the ornate handle on this vase.

Vase. #1183 — 6", semi-matte turquoise & brown wipe/ivory, $72.00 – 90.00. This color was also used on some of the Magnolia Line. It is much harder to find than the ivory & brown wipe. From the collection of Bev & Duane Brown.

Bowl. #1188 — 12", semi-matte turquoise & brown wipe/ivory, $68.00 – 80.00. These English Garden pieces were also made in an ivory and brown wipe, as shown previously, green and brown wipe, and yellow and brown wipe. From the collection of Bev & Duane Brown.

Candleholder. #1190 — 6", ivory/brown wipe, $22.00 – 28.00 each.

Candleholder. #1189 — 5", semi-matte green/brown wipe, $22.00 – 28.00 each.

Magnolia Group

    The Magnolia Group was the best selling of Red Wing's art pottery. This group was produced in the ivory wipe method and decorated with large magnolia flowers. Known to have been produced in brown, green, and yellow wipe, the colors other than brown are very hard to find. The group consisted of many different vases, bowls, and candleholders. There was also a small box with a lid and an ashtray made in Magnolia. You will notice that it is one of the loveliest groups in the art pottery lines.

Vase. #1012 — 7", ivory/brown wipe, handled pitcher vase, $58.00 – 75.00.

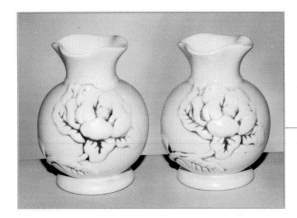

Vases. Pair #975 — 6", ivory/brown wipe, bulbous vases, $46.00 – 62.00 each.

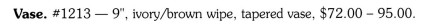

Vase. #1213 — 9", ivory/brown wipe, tapered vase, $72.00 – 95.00.

Vase. #1030 — 9", ivory/brown wipe, $78.00 – 100.00. This vase has the full view of the magnolia flower used on these pieces. It is interesting how they used different shaped flowers to fit the pottery, depending on the size and shape of the item.

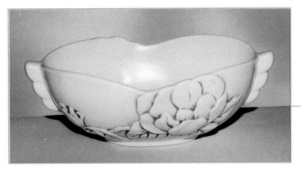

Bowl. #1016 — 10½", ivory/brown wipe, oblong wing handled bowl, $58.00 – 76.00. There is also a 12½" oval bowl.

Bowl. #1425 — 12", semi-matte ivory/brown wipe, $52.00 – 70.00.

Bowl. #1223 — 12½", ivory/brown wipe, oblong bowl, $72.00 – 95.00. Notice that this bowl has a very heavy wipe. On some items the brown wipe is hardly visible. This bowl and the previous ones were also part of a console set with candleholders.

Candleholders. Pair #1029 — 7", Magnolia candleholders, $48.00 – 65.00 each. These candleholders were quite expensive when originally sold in the 1930s for $24.00 a pair. Note the silver wing stamp on each candleholder. They were also part of a console set.

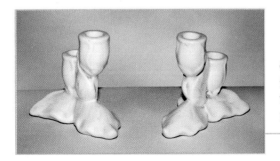

Candleholders. #1228 — 3", semi-matte ivory/brown wipe, $22.00 – 30.00 each. Some of the Red Wing candleholders you will not find in pairs. This is especially true with the vintage ones.

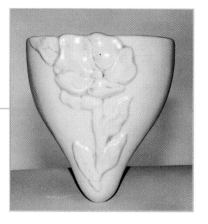

Wall Pocket. #1630 — 7", semi-matte ivory/brown wipe, $125.00 – 175.00. Wall pockets are very hard to find and command high prices.

Ashtray. #1019 — 4½", ivory/brown wipe, $42.00 – 60.00. This is one of the accessory pieces of the Magnolia Group, made so that you could have all matching pieces of a décor. There is also a small covered box, 4" x 3½", in this group. You do not often see these two items for sale.

Console Set. #1425 — 12" bowl, candleholders unmarked – 4", semi-matte ivory/brown wipe, Magnolia console set, $130.00 – 155.00. You will not find many console sets intact. When you can find them, the pricing is usually a little less than buying the individual pieces.

Console Set. #1223 — 12½" bowl, #1029 — 7½" candleholders, ivory/brown wipe, Magnolia console set, $150.00 – 195.00. A console set was also pictured with these candleholders and the large wing handled bowl in an original Red Wing catalog.

Renaissance Group

The Renaissance Group was also a popular line of pottery for Red Wing. Part of the Medallion Line, it consisted of vases, bowls, candleholders, and a centerpiece set. They were all quite ornate, done in the ivory wipe method and decorated with fancy style leaves. The centerpiece set consisted of a bowl and a frog insert that was a deer figurine. This set has come to be known as the Red Wing Stag. The deer centerpiece and the candleholders are the items most often seen. The vases and bowls are not often found.

Deer Insert Frog. #531 — 10", ivory/brown wipe, $45.00 – 60.00. Notice the holes in the base of the deer stand for flowers. The insert was put into the bowl with water and the flowers placed through the holes in the insert. These inserts, whatever shape, are called frogs.

Bowl. #526 — 12", ivory/brown wipe, centerpiece bowl, $45.00 – 60.00.

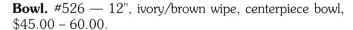

Candleholders. #529 — 6", ivory/brown wipe, $28.00 – 36.00 each. Notice some of the Red Wing candleholders looked more like small vases.

Centerpiece Set. #526 — 12" bowl, #531 — 10" deer insert, #529 – 6", candleholders, ivory/brown wipe, centerpiece set. $145.00 – 160.00. Centerpiece without candleholders, $98.00 – 120.00. The bowl and deer insert are known to have been produced in the 1950s in black, turquoise fleck, and zephyr pink fleck. These colors command higher prices.

Vintage Group

The Vintage Group was produced in a variety of vases, bowls, compotes, and candleholders. The pieces were covered in an ivory glaze and decorated with brown or color wipe. This group was decorated with grape clusters and leaves. The items were very ornate; some of the bowls were shaped like baskets with the grape vine handles. You will not see a lot of this group for sale.

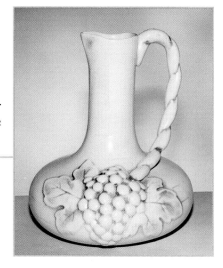

Vintage Urn. #616 — 11", semi-matte ivory/brown wipe, pitcher urn, $90.00 – 125.00. Notice the heavy brown wipe, which makes the grapes appear as a cluster.

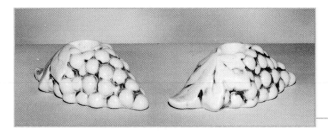

Vintage Candleholders. #622 — 5½" pair, semi-matte ivory/brown wipe, $22.00 – 30.00 each. Notice the grape leaf along with the cluster, which adds detail.

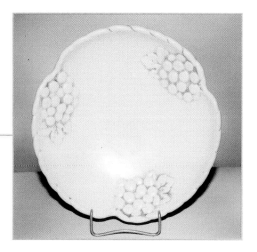

Vintage Bowl. #621 — 10", semi-matte ivory/brown wipe, $54.00 – 70.00.

Vintage Console Set. #624 — 10" bowl, #622 — 5½" candleholders, semi-matte ivory/brown wipe, console set, $98.00 – 130.00.

Miscellaneous

The original Red Wing catalogs always had some items listed as miscellaneous, and the following pieces fall in that category. Although not as ornate as some of the other pottery, they are part of the early line items.

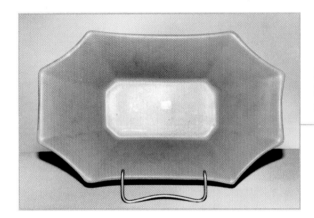

Bowl. #331 — 11", matte green, mandarin style, $52.00 – 65.00. This piece has the heavy matte finish of the first art pottery.

Pitcher. #50 — 8", semi-matte orange, $38.00 – 46.00. The inside was simply glazed stoneware. It originally came with a pottery and cork stopper in the same finish, not shown in this picture; the pricing given is without the stopper. A pitcher with original stopper would be priced $15.00 – 20.00 more.

Candleholders. #397 — 5½", ivory/brown wipe, $28.00 – 36.00 each.

Bowl. #279 — 9", semi-matte pink/ivory, scalloped edge, $48.00 – 60.00. The pink colored art pottery seems to command a higher price than some of the other colors. Note the silver wing stamp.

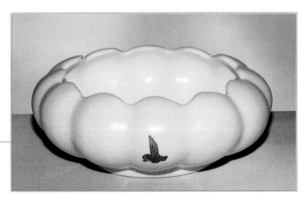

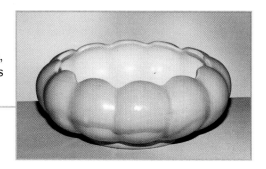

Bowl. #278 — 9", semi-matte green/ivory, scalloped edge, $38.00 – 46.00. Notice how the green glaze has run on this bowl. It almost seems to be a matte glaze that fired oddly.

Planter. #259 — 6", semi-matte, $54.00 – 68.00. This piece has a very heavy glaze, almost resembling a matte glaze. The swan planter was produced in later years and listed with the novelty planters.

Vase. #504 — 7½", turquoise matte/ivory, vase $48.00 – 62.00. This vase is very similar to a vase in the RumRill Line.

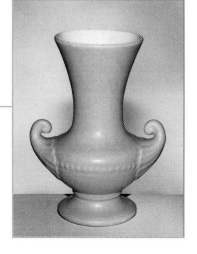

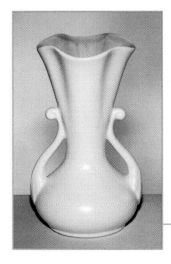

Vase. #505 — 7½", semi-matte ivory/green, $32.00 – 40.00. You will find this vase in many different colors. This shape was produced in both the early and the later years of art pottery.

RumRill Line

The RumRill Line was produced for a potter named, George Rumrill, who contracted Red Wing to produce his line of pottery from 1932 – 1937. The dates that the RumRill art ware was produced by Red Wing vary, but the 1932 – 1937 range is agreed upon by most. However, I have seen a Red Wing RumRill price list dated January 1938. Perhaps the line was discontinued in late 1937 or early 1938.

The pottery was bottom marked RumRill and numbered with the shape number. Quite a few of the RumRill pieces of art ware look identical to some of the Red Wing pottery since some of the same molds were used for both. Red Wing also used the same shape numbers on the bottom of some of the identical RumRill and Red Wing pieces.

The RumRill pottery is harder to find than the Red Wing, due to the short period of time that it was produced. Therefore, it commands higher prices than its Red Wing counterparts.

George Rumrill continued to produce his pottery at other plants after he left Red Wing. The pieces produced elsewhere are also bottom marked RumRill. However, you can tell the difference because they were marked in a different style. Some included a letter preceding the shape number, others had RumRill printed in all small letters. Most of the pottery produced somewhere other than Red Wing has "Made in the USA," or simply "USA" inscribed on the bottom along with the name and shape number.

The RumRill produced at Red Wing was bottom marked RumRill along with a shape number. Stickers were also used on some pieces, although they are not often found.

The pottery was produced in many styles of vases, bowls, and candleholders, along with specialty items. These were done in many different matte, semi-matte, and gloss finishes and colors. A list of some of these finishes is in the back of this book, along with a picture of the bottom marking used at Red Wing.

This art pottery is very popular today, not only with Red Wing collectors but also with RumRill collectors. A collection of RumRill is not only beautiful, but also gives a great deal of enjoyable searching.

Like Red Wing art ware, RumRill art pottery was produced in a number of different group names, each having its own theme. Among these groups were Grecian, Shell, Sylvan, Indian, Neo-Classic, Classic, and Mandarin. Several of the RumRill groups are shown in the following pictures.

Renaissance Group

The Renaissance group consisted of various vases, bowls, and a candlestick. All were decorated in the same leaf style. This group was produced in several finish colors.

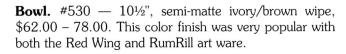

Vase. #522 — 6", semi-matte aqua/ivory, $52.00 – 74.00.

Bowl. #530 — 10½", semi-matte ivory/brown wipe, $62.00 – 78.00. This color finish was very popular with both the Red Wing and RumRill art ware.

Candleholder. #529 — 6", semi-matte crème/dark brown, $28.00 – 36.00 each. This candleholder has a sticker on the bottom that you would not usually find. The photo below shows that sticker.

Bottom Sticker on Candleholder. Although torn, the sticker states that this is shape #529 and finish #46. These stickers were probably used at the factory to enable workers to select the correct shape and finish for an order. These may have been placed on all items and removed before or after shipment.

Sylvan Group

The Sylvan group consisted of various style vases, bowls, and two different candleholders, along with a basket bowl. All were decorated in the same turned-out leaf style and done in a variety of finish colors.

Vase. #445 — 8", gloss coral/tan, $72.00 – 85.00. This color seems to be one that you could find. From the collection of Bev & Duane Brown.

Neo-Classic Group

The Neo-Classic group consisted of various style vases, bowls, and a candleholder produced in a variety of finish colors. All were decorated with ball handles. This line is very popular among collectors and is quite hard to find. The largest of the art ware pieces, a 15" vase #674, has been known to sell for up to $800.00.

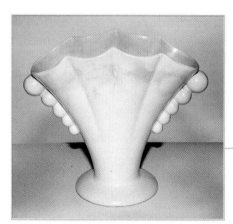

Vase. #668 — 10", semi-matte ivory/green, $175.00 – 225.00. You will find the ball handles on each piece of the Neo-Classic group in graduated sizes of five or six balls.

Indian Group

The Indian group consisted of vases, bowls, and a candleholder. There was also a pitcher with a matching stopper. Produced in various finish colors, the art ware had smooth lines with no decoration. Some of the pieces are known to have been finished with the famous Nokomis glaze. This was a semi-matte glaze in various shades of tan and olive, highlighted with a copper color. The art pottery with Nokomis is very rare and commands very high prices. You will not often see any art ware with this finish.

Vase. #291 — 5½", semi-matte ocean green, $55.00 – 72.00.

Bowl. #315 — 4½", semi-matte rose/aqua, $68.00 – 76.00.

Pitcher. #50 — 8", Gypsy orange, $56.00 – 62.00. This pitcher has an identical Red Wing counterpart pictured on page 32. The bottom stamp reads "RumRill" in blue ink, not the usual indented markings found on the Red Wing and RumRill pieces.

Grecian Group

The Grecian group consisted mostly of vases although there was a bowl with the same handles as the vase shown. This group was produced in smooth lines, some with circular handles. Finished in a variety of colors, there is also one shape in this group known to have been produced in the Nokomis finish.

Vase. #506 — 7½", semi-matte orange blend/tan, $68.00 – 75.00.

Classic Group

The Classic group consisted of vases, including a covered vase, bowls, candleholders, and also double and triple candelabra. Like the rest of the RumRill groups, the classic was produced in a variety of finishes. The finishes were changed in each price list with not all of them available at the same time.

Vase. #500 — 5½", semi-matte blue/white stippled, $75.00 – 90.00. This finish color was known as Dutch Blue on the RumRill price lists. It was finish #7 on the Red Wing lists. Notice the white spots on the blue, which were called stippled. This color is quite popular, today known as Dutch blue or stipple.

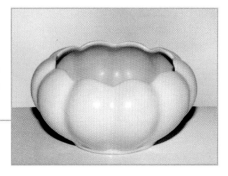

Bowl. #276 — 6", semi-matte eggshell/turquoise, $40.00 – 48.00. There is a bowl in the Red Wing line that is identical to this except for color.

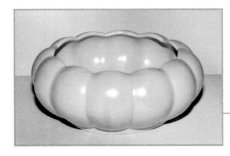

Bowl. #E12 — 7", semi-matte turquoise, $48.00 – 60.00. This bowl is an example of the quality work done at the Red Wing Pottery. Notice the perfect color and glaze on this piece.

Mandarin Group

This group came in a variety of vases and bowls; all have octagon shapes resembling a Greek style. The grouping is done in a matte glaze. It is hard to know the colors of this group, since the pieces are seldom seen.

Bowl. #331 — 12" matte green, $52.00 – 65.00. This bowl is identical to a Red Wing piece. Notice the heavy matte glaze.

Swan Group

The Swan group consisted of vases, bowls, planters, and urns. The swan appeared either as the handle or the body of the item. The colors known are plain pink and plain white done in a semi-matte glaze.

Planter. #259 — 6", semi-matte white, $42.00 – 55.00. Notice the partial RumRill stamp on this item. Although not intact, it shows that stamps were added to some of the RumRill pieces.

Shell Group

The Shell group was very ornate, consisting of vases, bowls, candelabra, and a handled dish made of three flat shells.

Vase. #432 — 7½", semi-matte ivory/pink, $68.00 – 82.00. Notice the intricate shell detail on this vase. All the pieces in this group were produced in elaborate detail.

Miscellaneous Group

The RumRill line has a group of miscellaneous items just like the Red Wing catalogs. Just as lovely as the named groups, several miscellaneous pieces are shown here.

Vase. #J10 & #H10 — 9½", semi-matte pink, handled vase, $62.00 – 89.00. This vase has an unusual double number marking. Perhaps two designers worked on this vase and both put their initials on the bottom marking.

Vase. #644 — 7", semi-matte ivory/matte blue, swirl vase, $68.00 – 80.00. This finish was #52 on the RumRill Art Pottery price list dated January 1938. Named Rivera, it was described as an ivory semi-matte, matte blue lined. As you can see, it is quite a striking finish.

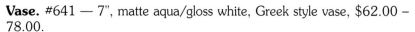

Vase. #641 — 7", matte aqua/gloss white, Greek style vase, $62.00 – 78.00.

Vase. #K8 — 12", semi-matte white, horn of plenty vase, $46.00 – 58.00.

Vase. #394 — 9", semi-matte turquoise/white, genie type vase, $62.00 – 80.00. The glaze on this piece is almost matte and it is identical to a Red Wing vase pictured on page 33.

Vase. #505 — 7½", semi-matte blue, miscellaneous vase, $52.00 – 68.00. Almost a baby blue color, this vase is very attractive. This shape number was carried throughout the production of Red Wing. This would be ideal for a collection of one piece in multiple colors.

Vase. #636 — 6½", semi-matte turquoise/gloss white, Egyptian style vase, $62.00 – 78.00.

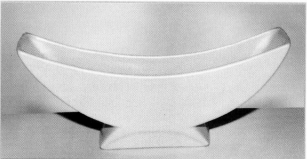

Bowl. #H18 — 11½", semi-matte pink, boat shaped bowl, $42.00 – 60.00.

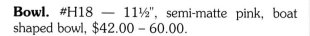

Bowl. #341 — 7", semi-matte ivory/matte blue, miscellaneous bowl, $68.00 – 76.00. This is also #52 Rivera finish.

Art Pottery 1940s

During the 1940s, Red Wing art pottery continued to be produced in a wide array of colors and adorned with decorations, although not quite as ornate as some of the early pottery. They also included considerable miscellaneous items and not as many line names.

Some of the early lines such as Magnolia and Renaissance were carried over into the 1940s production. This practice of adding some of the prior year's shapes to the new items produced continued through the 1950s and 1960s. Some of the pottery shapes carried through all the years of production, produced in a different finish in each era.

The items produced were vases, bowls, compotes, and cornucopias. There were also candleholders, planters, and console sets, along with specialty items, all produced in a variety of plain and two tone colors in different glazes.

Vases

Vase. #1160 — 9½", gloss luster blue/coral, leaf motif vase, $58.00 – 72.00. This would be a good choice for those who want to arrange their collection by color. There were numerous pieces produced with this finish, many of them very decorative. As you can see, it is quite a lovely finish.

Vase. #1169 — 7½", semi-matte ivory/green, ribbon vase, $46.00 – 68.00. This vase was also produced in 8½" and 9½". It is one of the items which continued through the 1950s and 1960s with the same shape number in different colors.

Vase. #946 — 6", semi-matte white, fan-shaped small vase, $28.00 – 36.00.

Vase. #1174 — 7", semi-matte pink/ivory, leaf embossed vase, $48.00 – 62.00.

Vase. #884 — 10", semi-matte white, footed vase, $48.00 – 65.00. Simple but elegant, this vase would look good in any setting.

Vase. #110 — 7½", semi-matte burnt orange/gray, rose decorated vase, $62.00 – 80.00. The dark spots you see on this vase are gold blotches in the finish. This is quite an unusual finish, not seen often. From the collection of Bev & Duane Brown.

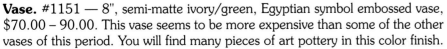

Vase. #1151 — 8", semi-matte ivory/green, Egyptian symbol embossed vase, $70.00 – 90.00. This vase seems to be more expensive than some of the other vases of this period. You will find many pieces of art pottery in this color finish.

Vase. #1115 — 7¼", semi-matte green/ivory, leaf embossed vase, $52.00 – 68.00.

Vase. #1162 — 9", gloss gray/yellow, decorator purple leaf trimmed vase, $68.00 – 80.00. The decorator pieces have contrasting colors on the trim. This shape was also produced in plain colors. The decorator vases would be an excellent selection for a color collection. They were produced in a wide variety of shapes and colors. From the collection of Bev & Duane Brown.

Vase. No number — 12", semi-matte ivory/green, fan type vase, $38.00 – 46.00. This vase is unusual with no bottom shape number. The marking simply reads "Red Wing." Perhaps this is a sample item, although sample items have been found marked as such with "Sample" on the bottom. It is identical to a vase in the Manhattan group, #537 — 12". However with no shape number, it cannot be identified as such.

Vase. #982 — 7½", semi-matte ivory/green, fan vase, $36.00 – 48.00. This piece was also produced through the 1950s and 1960s. It would make a good selection for a collection of one item in different colors because it was produced in every color imaginable, offering a wide selection. Also, they are easier to find and more affordable than some of the other pieces.

Vase. #1103 — 8½", gloss tan/green, decorator brown leaf trimmed vase, $48.00 – 64.00. From the collection of Bev & Duane Brown.

Vase. #1377 — 10", semi-matte aqua/ivory, oil lamp style vase, $75.00 – 95.00. From the collection of Bev & Duane Brown.

Vase. #M1442 — 8½", semi-matte ivory/green, snifter vase, $52.00 – 70.00. Also produced in the 1950s and 1960s. Note the silver wing label.

Vase. #1170 — 6¾", semi-matte ivory/green, sawtooth vase, $42.00 – 50.00. Also produced in the 1950s and 1960s.

Vase. #1377 — 10", semi-matte maroon/gray, oil lamp style vase, $85.00 – 110.00. This maroon finish in any piece of art ware commands higher prices. From the collection of Bev & Duane Brown.

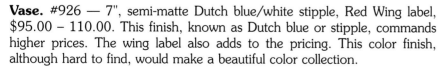

Vase. #926 — 7", semi-matte Dutch blue/white stipple, Red Wing label, $95.00 – 110.00. This finish, known as Dutch blue or stipple, commands higher prices. The wing label also adds to the pricing. This color finish, although hard to find, would make a beautiful color collection.

Vase. #1360 — 7½", semi-matte ivory/green, flower embossed vase, $36.00 – 48.00. Front of vase is shown at the top of next page in a different color combination.

Vase. #1097 — 5¾", semi-matte ivory/green, ivy decorated cornucopia vase, $38.00 – 46.00.

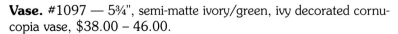

Vase. #886 — 7½", semi-matte orange/tan tulip shaped vase, $38.00 – 46.00. This vase was also produced in shape #885 — 9½" size which looked the same.

Vase. #1155 — 10", semi-matte ivory/green, leaf embossed vase, $48.00 – 60.00.

Vase. #871 — 7½", semi-matte ivory/green, trophy vase, $38.00 – 50.00. This vase would make a good color collection since it was also produced through the 1950s and 1960s in a variety of colors. It was also finished in the zephyr pink fleck, which commands a higher price.

Vase. #1360 — 7½", semi-matte green/ivory, flower embossed vase, $36.00 – 48.00. This is the front view of the same shape vase on page 44.

Vase. #1111 — 7½", semi-matte pink/ivory, double handled vase, $48.00 – 62.00.

Vase. #1204 — 10", gloss yellow/gray, brown leaf trimmed vase, $48.00 – 65.00. From the collection of Bev & Duane Brown.

Vase. #1107 — 7", gloss gray/yellow, purple flower trimmed decorator vase, $58.00 – 70.00. From the collection of Bev & Duane Brown.

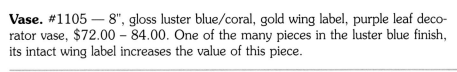

Vase. #1105 — 8", gloss luster blue/coral, gold wing label, purple leaf decorator vase, $72.00 – 84.00. One of the many pieces in the luster blue finish, its intact wing label increases the value of this piece.

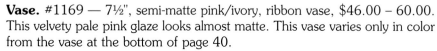

Vase. #1356 — 7½", semi-matte green/ivory, snail shaped vase, $32.00 – 42.00. The outside glaze, which looks almost like a matte, has fired through to the inside ivory, making spots of green on the inside of the vase.

Vase. #1169 — 7½", semi-matte pink/ivory, ribbon vase, $46.00 – 60.00. This velvety pale pink glaze looks almost matte. This vase varies only in color from the vase at the bottom of page 40.

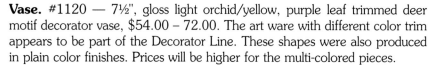

Vase. #1202 — 10½", pink/ivory, leaf motif vase, $36.00 – 44.00. This vase has the look of some of the earlier pieces.

Vase. #1120 — 7½", gloss light orchid/yellow, purple leaf trimmed deer motif decorator vase, $54.00 – 72.00. The art ware with different color trim appears to be part of the Decorator Line. These shapes were also produced in plain color finishes. Prices will be higher for the multi-colored pieces.

Vase. #1102 — 8", gloss luster blue/coral, purple leaf trimmed decorator vase, $62.00 – 75.00. The luster blue pieces are harder to find than some of the other colors. From the collection of Bev & Duane Brown.

Vase. #1159 — 8", semi-matte pink/ivory, embossed vase, $72.00 – 86.00. You will find that this pink and ivory finish is higher priced, perhaps because it is harder to find. The embossed finish also adds value. From the collection of Bev & Duane Brown.

Vase. #889 — 8", semi-matte ivory/green, flower embossed vase, $58.00 – 68.00. This finish is another good one to collect if you are going to organize your collection by color. You will find a wide array of shape numbers in this color.

Vase. #1053 — 8", semi-matte green/ivory, trophy style vase, $42.00 – 55.00.

Vase. #1237 — 8", semi-matte pink/ivory, footed vase, $48.00 – 56.00.

Vase. #887 — 7½", semi-matte pink/ivory, flared top vase, $56.00 – 67.00. From the collection of Bev & Duane Brown.

Vase. #880 — 8", semi-matte ivory/green, tapered vase, $48.00 – 56.00. From the collection of Bev & Duane Brown.

Vase. #1107 — 7½", matte green/ivory, leaf embossed vase, $56.00 – 68.00.

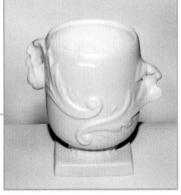

Vase. #929 — 10", semi-matte ivory/brown wipe, leaf trimmed vase, $62.00 – 78.00.

Vase. #1096 — 9", semi-matte ivory/brown wipe, leaf motif vase, $72.00 – 84.00. The brown wipe finish commands higher prices because it is quite hard to find. This finish was produced by applying a brown stain to the ivory finish and then wiping off the excess, leaving the brown color in the recessed parts of the trim. As you can see, this created a lovely piece of art ware. This is the same finish seen on the Magnolia group pictured earlier. Some art ware was produced with a green wipe, and these green wipe pieces are quite rare and hardly ever found.

Vase. #1240 — 5", semi-matte pink/ivory, cornucopia type vase, $48.00 – 56.00.

Vase. #952 — 6", gloss blue, swirl vase, $48.00 – 60.00. Although simple, this is a very lovely vase.

Vase. #1056 — 9½", semi-matte ivory/green, gold wing label, urn type vase, $68.00 – 76.00 without lid. Any vases with lids are not often found intact. When found with the lid, the vase is worth considerably more. A pair of these vases along with the bowl #1055 — 12" were pictured in the 1940s Red Wing catalog as a console set. The bowl has the same handles as the vase. Below is a view of this vase with the lid on.

Vase. #1056 — 9½", semi-matte ivory/green, urn type vase, $84.00 – 98.00 with lid.

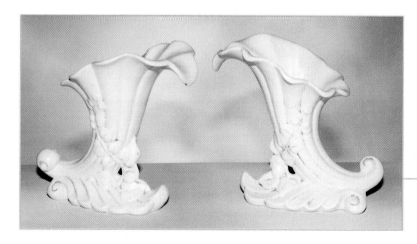

Vases. Pair #1098 — 8½", semi-matte ivory/brown wipe, cornucopia vases, $42.00 – 58.00 each.

Bowls

Bowl. #1322 — 5½", semi-matte ivory/brown wipe bowl, $38.00 – 54.00.

Bowl. #1241 — 5", gloss luster blue/coral, leaf embossed bowl, $52.00 – 68.00. You will notice that the luster blue and coral finish tends to vary in color. This is because the colors were mixed by hand and would vary slightly with each production run. You will find this is also true with the ivory and green finish. From the collection of Bev & Duane Brown.

Bowl. #1037 — 8", gloss luster blue/coral, square bowl, $38.00 – 46.00. You will not find many bowls of this vintage, because there were not a lot produced in the earlier art ware. Later in the 1950s and 1960s many types of bowls were produced and are readily found.

Bowl. #276 — 6", semi-matte ivory/mustard marble, classic style bowl, $42.00 – 56.00. Notice the marble finish inside this bowl. It is quite unusual.

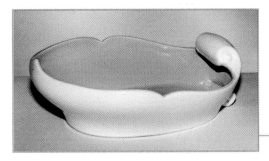

Bowl. #1092 — 10½", semi-matte ivory/green, Garden Club style bowl, $32.00 –40.00. This style of bowl is very similar to the Garden Club bowls produced in the 1960s, shown beginning on page 97.

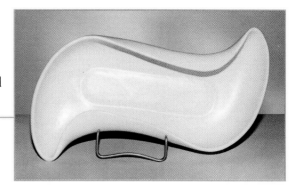

Bowl. #M1447 — 12½", semi-matte ivory, contoured bowl, $28.00 – 36.00.

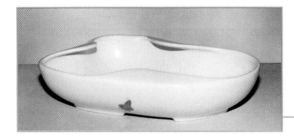

Bowl. #899 — 6½", semi-matte ivory, small footed bowl, silver wing label, $30.00 – 38.00. Although this piece has a wing label on it, the label is in bad shape and does not add to the value of the bowl.

Bowl. #1620 — 10", semi-matte ivory, silver wing label, scallop edge console bowl, $40.00 – 50.00. Notice the perfect wing label on this piece. This bowl is part of a console set shown on page 54.

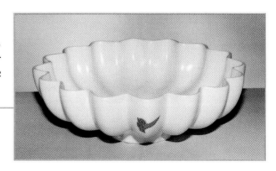

Bowl. #426 — 10¾", semi-matte green/ivory, scallop edge flat bowl, $32.00 – 40.00. Shown at left is the inside of this bowl, and below is the outside. This was a particularly flat piece of pottery, which limited its uses.

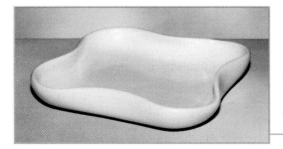

Bowl. #1037 — 7½", semi-matte pink, square bowl, $30.00 – 38.00. This is the same pale pink as the ribbon vase pictured on page 46.

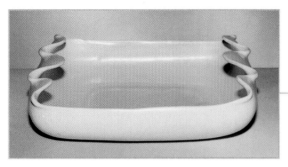

Bowl. #1409 — 8½", semi-matte ivory/green, ribbon edge bowl, $32.00 – 38.00.

Bowl. #M1492 — 9½", semi-matte ivory, round footed bowl, $30.00 – 38.00. This bowl was ideal for floating flowers.

Compotes

Compote. #M1597 — 7", semi-matte ivory, compote with medium pedestal, $30.00 – 36.00.

Compote. #690 — 9", semi-matte ivory, fluted compote, $42.00 – 56.00. This compote was also produced in the 1960s in Red Wing's Stereoline. It was a very attractive piece.

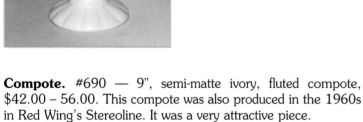

Planters

Planter. #770 — 7½", semi-matte ivory/green, silver wing label, ribbed planter, $32.00 – 40.00. The planters of the 1940s vintage, done in this finish, were quite elegant.

Planter. #1195 — 5", semi-matte ivory/green, round flower handled planter, $34.00 – 42.00. This was the planter that belonged to my mother which led me to begin collecting Red Wing.

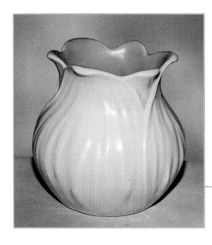

Planter. #896 — 7", semi-matte yellow/turquoise, tulip shaped planter, $38.00 – 46.00. This planter also came in a 4" size. The color is different than most 1940s items. This piece almost has the look of a Rum-Rill item.

Candleholders

Candleholders. #1619 — 4½", semi-matte ivory, scallop edge, $30.00 – 40.00 pair. Most of the candleholders of this vintage were quite fancy and sold for quite a lot of money for the times, ranging from $12.00 to $42.00 per pair in the Red Wing catalogs.

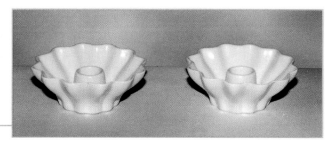

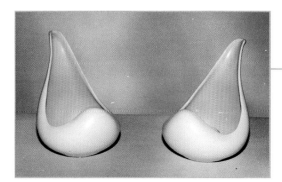

Candleholders. #B1409 — 5", semi-matte ivory/green, teardrop shape, $22.00 – 30.00 pair.

Candleholders. Pair #1286 — 8", gloss turquoise, leaf motif, $30.00 – 38.00 each. Called candlesticks in the Red Wing catalogs, they are harder to find than other art ware.

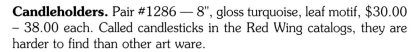

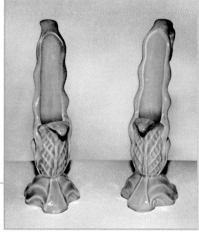

Centerpieces

Centerpiece. #1037 — 8" bowl, unmarked bird figurine — 5", gloss luster blue/coral set, $75.00 – 90.00.

Console Sets

Console Set. Bowl #1620 — 10", #1619 — 4½" candleholders, semi-matte ivory, scallop edge set, $80.00 – 110.00.

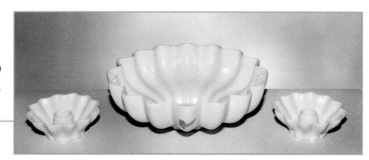

Wall Pockets

Wall pockets make a beautiful and unique collection. They are quite hard to find, but worth the search. You will find them to be more expensive than some of the other art ware because they are quite scarce. This would also be a good collection for someone with limited space, as your collection could be hung on the walls and flowers can be added to match your décor.

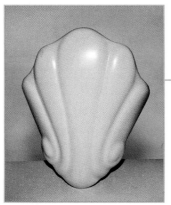

Wall Pocket. #1254 — 7", semi-matte pink/ivory, sconce type, $72.00 – 95.00. Wall pockets of any kind are very hard to find.

Figurines

Figurine. Unmarked — 5", gloss coral/faint blue, bird figurine, $46.00 – 60.00. Part of the centerpiece shown above. Although unmarked, this figurine is advertised as Red Wing. There is also a larger size.

Novelty Pieces

The art pottery of the 1940s had a variety of novelty pieces. There were assorted animal planters and miniature vases and bowls. Although not readily found, these novelty pieces would make a very nice collection.

Vase. #873 — 4", semi-matte yellow, miniature, $60.00 – 75.00. It is hard to imagine what they put in these tiny vases. It is thought that many of these novelty items were made for use in a child's room.

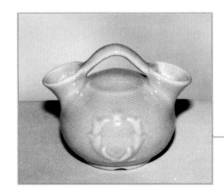

Vase. #908 – 4", gloss pink, double hole miniature, $60.00 – 75.00.

Planter. #1338 — 5½", gloss turquoise deer planter, $85.00 – 100.00. Other animal planters included a horse, seal, teddy bear, duck, pig, rabbit, and fish. There were also some fruit shaped planters.

Planter. No bottom mark — 6½", matte blue, silver wing label, lamb planter, $110.00 – 145.00. Shown in a 1948 Red Wing catalog, this planter is known to have also been produced in matte gray, yellow, ivory, and green. Any of these animal planters is quite rare.

Art Pottery 1950s

As Red Wing entered the 1950s and 1960s production eras, they introduced a wide array of colors along with a contemporary look in a lot of the art ware, a departure from the traditional colors and shapes they used in the 1930s and 1940s.

As in previous years, some of the 1930s and 1940s art ware shapes were carried into the new production period. In the mid-1950s Red Wing introduced a variety of new art pottery, all done in a gloss glaze, most with the Art Deco look and style. The colors ranged from the traditional white to orchid, produced in a wide variety of oddly-shaped pieces. Some of the art pottery of this period is not as easily recognized by sight as was the earlier art ware. But once you become familiar with some of the new colors and shapes, recognition will be easier.

Continuing the trend started in the 1940s, the 1950s art pottery did not use a lot of line names. Pieces were grouped in the Red Wing catalogs by items, such as vases, bowls, compotes, and planters, along with a miscellaneous section following each grouping. The candleholders, which were called candlesticks in the earlier catalogs, were usually grouped on a page with a matching console bowl, and were sold to form a console set. Many varieties of ashtrays, a cake salver, and large contemporary cornucopias were also introduced.

Along with these items they continued with the novelty planters, and also introduced some unique music motif planters, among them a banjo, violin, and a piano, all produced in detail to resemble the real musical instruments. The violins can be found more often than the others and are still affordable. A piano planter found in excellent condition can command up to $500 depending on the color. There is also a cart planter with movable brass wheels.

The colors of the art pottery line were broadened to include a wide array of bright glossy finishes. They also continued the plain two-tone finishes. Introduced in the mid-1950s was a line of fleck colors. The color was flecked with a light black or brown and was used on solid fleck art ware as well as two-tone. On the two-tone pieces, the fleck color was usually used on the outside with a solid color finish on the inside.

There are several of these fleck colors, fleck yellow, fleck green, fleck zephyr pink, fleck Nile blue, and fleck orchid. The art ware done in these colors was quite attractive and modern looking. Although harder to find, these finishes would be a good choice for a collection organized by color. You will find the blue and pink fleck most often.

As you will see from the following pictures, the look and colors of the art ware during this period were changing with the times.

Vases

Vase. #M3007 — 12", semi-matte burnt orange, jug type, $58.00 – 70.00. This shape number is shown as part of the Decorator Line done in crystalline glazes in the Red Wing catalog for fall 1959. However the number is not preceded with the M, which is the designer's, Charles Murphy, initial. Therefore, it is not certain that it was part of that line. The pricing would be a lot higher if that could be confirmed. A vase from the Decorator Line with a silver green finish has been known to sell for several hundred dollars. From the collection of Bev & Duane Brown.

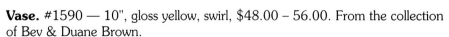

Vase. #1590 — 10", gloss yellow, swirl, $48.00 – 56.00. From the collection of Bev & Duane Brown.

Vase. #505 — 7½", gloss fleck orchid/semi-matte orchid, fluted top, $42.00 – 58.00. This shape number is one that was produced starting in the 1930s and carried on through the 1960s. You will find a variety of different colors on this piece of art ware. This piece would make a good choice if you wanted to organize your collection with one item in a wide array of colors.

Vase. #871 — 7½", gloss maroon/gray, trophy style, $46.00 – 58.00.

Vase. #1120 — 9", semi-matte cypress green, compote, $38.00 – 52.00. This vase was also produced in the 1960s and placed in the Floraline section in the 1960s catalogs.

Vase. #M1439 — 6", semi-matte white/green, leaf footed, $42.00 – 54.00.

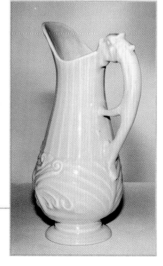

Vase. #220 — 10", gloss yellow/gray, fish handled pitcher vase, $90.00 – 120.00. This vase was also produced in the 1940s with different finish colors. A maroon vase in this shape number is known to have sold for $375.00. You will not often find these vases, and the price will be determined by the vintage and finish color. From the collection of Bev & Duane Brown.

Vase. #220 — 10", gloss fleck Nile blue/colonial buff, fish handled pitcher vase, $98.00 – 130.00. From the collection of Bev & Duane Brown.

Vase. #1196 — 10", gloss gray/yellow, purple flower handled, $48.00 – 62.00. This vase has the look of the earlier Decorator Line, perhaps carried over to the 1950s.

Vase. #686 — 12", gloss buff/ light celadon, silver wing label, bulbous cylinder type, $48.00 – 56.00. This shape number was used several times by Red Wing. There is a vase with this number in the 1930s miscellaneous and also in the 1960s Chromoline. They are identical in shape, only the finishes are different. From the collection of Bev & Duane Brown.

Vase. #357 — 8", gloss gray/coral, leaf trimmed, footed, $38.00 – 46.00. From the collection of Bev & Duane Brown.

Vase. #1168 — 7", semi-matte ivory/green, flat handled, $42.00 – 56.00.

Vase. #1295 — 7", semi-matte orange/ivory, shell type, $36.00 – 48.00.

Vase. #1202 — 5½", gloss blue/coral, contoured, $34.00 – 42.00.

Vase. #B1397 — 7", gloss gray/coral, tapered, $32.00 – 40.00.

Vase. #M1457 — 7½", gloss fleck yellow, spike trimmed, $42.00 – 56.00.

Vase. #1625 — 10", semi-matte salmon/yellow, petal shaped, $44.00 – 56.00.

Vase. #1556 — 6", gloss fleck zephyr pink, cloverleaf shape, $38.00 – 44.00.

Vase. #505 — 7½", gloss blue/pink, cloverleaf shape, $32.00 – 40.00. This vase and number were also produced in the 1930s and continued in a variety of colors on through the 1960s.

Vase. #M1442 — 8½", gloss fleck yellow, snifter type, $46.00 – 58.00. This is one of the new fleck colors introduced and is harder to find. This vase was also produced in the 1940s in semi-matte ivory.

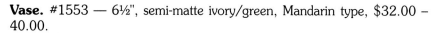

Vase. #1553 — 6½", semi-matte ivory/green, Mandarin type, $32.00 – 40.00.

Vase. #892 — 7½", semi-matte ivory/green, fan style, $38.00 – 46.00. Shown in the traditional semi-matte ivory, the fan vase was produced through the 1960s.

Vase. #1356 — 7½", gloss pea green/brown, snail shaped, $30.00 – 38.00.

Vase. #1169 — 7½", semi-matte ivory/green, ribbon style, $42.00 – 58.00. Sold from the 1940s through the 1960s, the green is a different shade than on the 1940s vase.

Vase. #1097 — 5¾", gloss blue/yellow, silver wing label, cornucopia vase, $36.00 – 48.00. Sold in a semi-matte ivory in the 1940s.

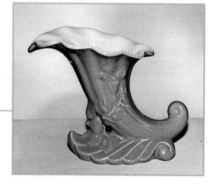

Vase. #M5000 — 8", semi-matte cocoa brown, urn type, $30.00 – 38.00. This vase has the look of the 1930s vintage pottery.

Vase. #1162 — 9", gloss pea green/gray, vine handled, $48.00 – 60.00. This vase was also part of a decorator line in the late 1930s, done in ivory with green vine decorations.

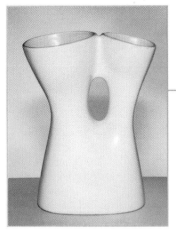

Vase. #B1427 — 8", semi-matte ivory/green, gladiolus shaped, $32.00 – 46.00. This is one of the new type vases introduced in the 1950s. It was designed especially for gladiola flowers.

Vase. #B1425 — 8", gloss burnt orange/green, contemporary style, $30.00 – 38.00.

Bowls

Monarch Line

The Monarch Line consisted of two patterns, Gothic and Contemporary. Advertised in the Red Wing catalog as a line of planters and low bowls. Monarch also has one vase in each pattern. Pictured following is the Gothic pattern; the Contemporary pattern is similar in color but has a stripe design.

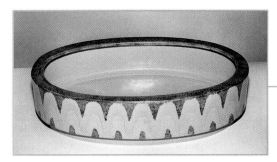

Bowl. #937 — 10", semi-matte green/brown trim, Gothic, $40.00 – 52.00.

Bowl. #1372 — 11", gloss maroon/ivory crackle, contoured bowl, $38.00 – 48.00. Although hard to see, the inside of this bowl has a crackle finish.

Bowl. #414 — 7", gloss brown/orange, flat bowl, $32.00 – 44.00.

Bowl. #M1448 — 8", gloss gray/yellow, character embossed bowl, $38.00 – 46.00.

Bowl. #1264 — 9", semi-matte ivory/green, large top tapered bowl, $44.00 – 56.00. Notice the brown spot inside this bowl. The brown color was fired with the inside glaze, perhaps a mistake or a blended glaze.

Bowl. #M1567 — 9", gloss fleck Nile blue, shell bowl, $44.00 – 56.00. This another example of the different pieces of art ware in the fleck Nile blue color. From the collection of Bev & Duane Brown.

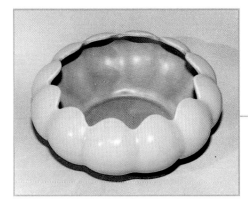

Bowl. #278 — 9", gloss yellow/gray, classic type bowl, $40.00 – 52.00. From the collection of Bev & Duane Brown.

Bowl. #835 — 8", matte white, low concave bowl, $35.00 – 46.00. This bowl is rounded inside and very shallow.

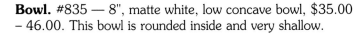

Bowl. #1251 — 12", gloss luster blue/coral, leaf shape bowl, $42.00 – 54.00. This bowl has a detailed vein on the inside and bottom.

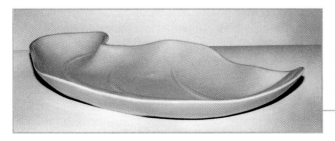

Bowl. #5015 — 9", matte gray, rectangular bowl, $30.00 – 38.00.

Bowl. #1382 — 12", gloss gray/coral, boat type bowl, $35.00 – 42.00.

Bowl. #M1535 — 4", gloss brown/turquoise, silver wing label, triangular hand-painted bowl, $38.00 – 48.00. The colors on the inside of this bowl were hand painted. The wing label is quite faded and does not add much value to this item.

Bowl. #M1537 — 4", gloss brown/turquoise, round hand-painted bowl, $38.00 – 48.00. A counterpart to the bowl above, this inside was also hand painted. Notice the lines are different from the first bowl's.

Bowl. #1620 — 10", semi-matte salmon, scallop-edged bowl, $42.00 – 56.00. This bowl was advertised as a console bowl in the Red Wing catalog. There were matching candleholders to form the set.

Bowl. #1483 — 18", fleck zephyr pink, spiked bowl, $48.00 – 60.00. This bowl sold for $6.00 in the fall 1957 Red Wing catalog, which was one of the higher priced items of that time. From the collection of Bev & Duane Brown.

Bowl. #5019 — 9", semi-matte green, rectangular bowl, $30.00 – 38.00. Elegant in the semi-matte green color, it almost seems to have a touch of gloss in the glaze.

Compotes

Compote. #5022 — 7", fleck Nile blue/colonial buff, gold wing label, modern style, $48.00 – 60.00.

Compote. #5011 — 4½" x 6¾", semi-matte green, pedestal style, $30.00 – 36.00. Like the rectangular bowl above with same finish, this is a very elegant looking compote.

Candleholders

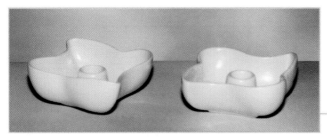

Candleholders. #B1411 — 4", semi-matte ivory, petal-shaped, $24.00 – 30.00 pair. These candleholders were also part of a console set with a bowl of the same shape, set shown on page 68.

Candleholders. #1619 — 4½", semi-matte salmon, scallop-edged candleholders, $32.00 – 40.00 pair. These candleholders were part of a console set with bowl #1620 shown on page 64.

Candleholders. #B1411 – 4", gloss gray/coral, petal-shaped, $26.00 – 34.00 pair. These are the same shape candleholders pictured above with a different finish.

Decorator Brass Line

Introduced in 1958, this was the only line produced by Red Wing to be trimmed in brass. There were several styles of vases, planters, and compotes. Produced in a variety of color finishes including black and the fleck colors, this was very attractive art ware, and tends to be higher in price because of its scarcity.

Vase. #M1609 — 10", semi-matte ivory, brass-handled vase, $46.00 – 60.00. The handles on all the vases were leaf shaped. The brass was attached with screws through a hole drilled into the pottery.

Compote. #M1598 — 8", semi-matte ivory, medium pedestal, brass handled, $48.00 – 60.00.

Planter. #M1612 — 10½" x 4¾", gloss fleck yellow, brass-trimmed, $42.00 – 56.00.

Decorator Glazed Line

Two of the different decorator lines of the 1950s were produced in crystalline and crackle glazes. These glazes were accomplished by firing the pottery in different stages, firing the next glaze then covering the crackle or crystalline with another finish and firing again. It was quite a complicated process, but produced a totally different look to the pottery.

The crystalline art ware is known to have been produced in vases and ashtrays. The finishes used were blue, silver-green, and orange. Not often found, this art ware tends to be quite expensive.

Vase. #1301 — 5", gloss blue/gun metal, crackle vase, $48.00 – 60.00. The glaze on this vase was fired in three stages and produced a very unique look.

Console Sets

Console Set. #M1483 — 18" bowl, #B1411 — 4" candleholders, fleck zephyr pink console set, $72.00 – 98.00. Candleholders sold separately, $32.00 – 40.00 pair. There is also a pair of spike trimmed candleholders that go with this bowl. From the collection of Bev & Duane Brown.

Console Set. #278 — 9" bowl, #1308 — 10" figurine, gloss yellow/gray classic type console set, $145.00 – 175.00. The figurine in this set is very expensive and makes the total price quite high. The figurine alone is shown on page 73. From the collection of Bev & Duane Brown.

Console Set. #1620 — 10" bowl, #1619 — 4½" candleholders, semi-matte salmon, scallop-edged console set, $68.00 – 80.00.

Console Set. #B1391 — 8" bowl, #B1411 — 4" candleholders, gloss gray/coral petal-shaped console set, $58.00 – 72.00.

Planters

The following pieces of art ware were some of the many planters produced in the 1950s. People must have used a lot of planters in their homes considering the many different kinds that were produced, including novelty planters. They came in all different shapes, designs, and colors. When looking for Red Wing planters, you almost have to look at the bottom of any planter to determine if it is Red Wing; you cannot tell most of them just by appearance.

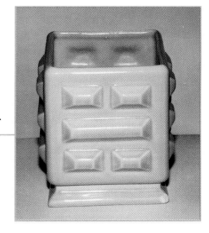

Planter. #1378 — 5½", gloss gray/coral, square planter, $32.00 – 45.00.

Planter. #1552 — 6", fleck yellow/light green, shelf planter, $28.00 – 36.00.

Planter. #970 — 3½", gloss aqua, small rimmed planter, $24.00 – 36.00. These planters produced since the 1940s were called flowerpots in the early catalogs.

Planter. #677 — 8½", gloss gray/coral, leaf embossed planter, $28.00 – 36.00.

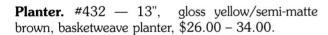

Planter. #677 — 4½", gloss orange/light green, leaf embossed planter, $24.00 – 32.00. This planter style, like the previous one, also came in a 6" size.

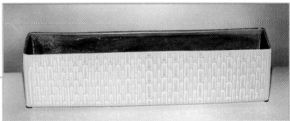

Planter. #432 — 13", gloss yellow/semi-matte brown, basketweave planter, $26.00 – 34.00.

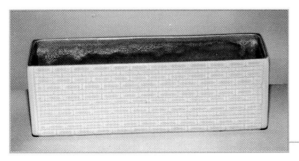

Planter. #431 — 10", gloss yellow/semi-matte brown, basketweave planter, $24.00 – 32.00. Except for size, this planter is identical to the one above.

Planter. #1278 — 4½", gloss yellow/metallic brown, small embossed planter, $30.00 – 42.00. The art ware finished with the metallic brown color is hard to find. Quite attractive, you will find it is higher priced.

Planter. #643 — 4", gloss fleck zephyr pink, round embossed planter, $34.00 – 40.00.

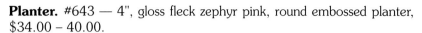

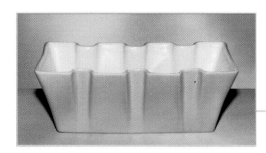

Planter. #1265 — 10", semi-matte green/ivory, Greek style planter, $28.00 – 34.00. By this period, very few pieces of art ware were produced in the semi-matte glaze. However, Red Wing continued to use this glaze on a few items through the 1960s.

Planter. #M1549 — 7", semi-matte ivory/green, rectangular footed planter, $20.00 – 26.00.

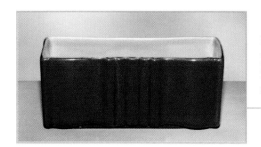

Planter. #1572 — 7", gloss maroon/light gray, rectangular planter, $38.00 – 45.00. This maroon color seems to be higher in price than some of the other colors of this vintage. There are also candleholders known to have been produced in the color.

Planter. #1616 — 7½", semi-matte green, grid embossed planter, $34.00 – 40.00.

Novelty Planters

Introduced in the late 1950s was a very unique line of novelty planters. They included a baby grand piano, a violin, a banjo, and a cart. These planters were done in great detail to be realistic. The planters were done in a variety of solid and flecked colors.

Planter. #M1484 — 13", gloss zephyr pink fleck, violin planter, $45.00 – 55.00. Notice they added rubber band strings to add realism. The banjo also had rubber band strings.

Planter. #1484 — 13", semi-matte black, violin planter, $48.00 – 58.00. Art ware done in the black color is harder to find and commands higher prices. Again notice the rubber band strings.

Planter. #M1525 — 10" x 9", gloss fleck yellow, baby grand piano planter, $240.00 – 350.00. The piano planters are one of the most sought after items in the art pottery. In good condition, they command very high prices. The piano was also produced in black, which sells for considerably more than the other colors. Notice the detail on these pianos. As you can see, they even put little black and white keys on them. The top of the piano is removable.

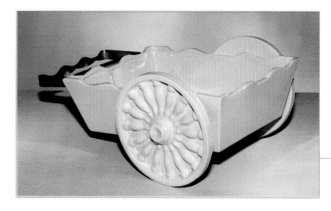

Planter. #M1531 — 9" x 7", semi-matte celadon yellow, cart planter, $45.00 – 70.00. As with the other planters, the cart was done in detail. Notice the brass handle. The wheels also go around.

Wall Pockets

Wall Pocket. #M1630 — 10", semi-matte cypress green, funnel-shaped wall pocket, $80.00 – 110.00. Very hard to find, any of the Red Wing wall pockets command high prices.

Wall Pocket. #441 — 6", gloss fleck Nile blue/colonial buff, cornucopia wall pocket, $75.00 – 90.00. This wall pocket matches the cornucopias that follow.

Cornucopias

Although harder to find than some of the other art ware, a collection of cornucopias would be quite unique. You could also include the cornucopia-shaped vases produced earlier.

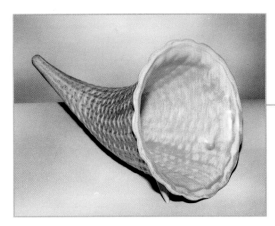

Cornucopia. #443 — 10", gloss fleck Nile blue/colonial buff, $52.00 – 68.00.

Cornucopia. #442 — 15", gloss fleck Nile blue/colonial buff, $68.00 – 80.00.

Figurines

Figurines would make a beautiful collection. They would also be good for collectors with limited space to store or display their art ware. Although you will find them very expensive and quite hard to locate, this would be a great collection. There were many different people figurines, among them a cowboy, cherubs, a Madonna, and an Oriental man and woman.

Figurine. #1308 — 10", gloss yellow, Oriental woman figurine, $100.00 – 130.00. There was also a matching man figurine. From the collection of Bev & Duane Brown.

Art Pottery 1960s

In the early 1960s, Red Wing continued grouping their art pottery by item in their catalogs. Some of the shapes from the past were carried on, as had been done in previous years.

During this period Red Wing went back to the style of giving line names to their art pottery. This practice gave the art ware a certain distinction as it did with the older lines. Some of the new lines were Floraline, Stereoline, and Chromoline. They also introduced a new Decorator Line and a Deluxe Line in the 1960s. These lines were quite ornate like some of their earlier counterparts. Also introduced were a Prismatique Line, a Belle Line, and a Bronze Line. You will see examples of these in this chapter.

The colors of the 1960s continued toward bright and modern, but Red Wing gave them more specific names, such as cypress green, sagebrush, hyacinth, butterscotch, orchid, and coral. They did, however, continue the basic colors that had been seen in earlier years.

The Red Wing catalogs of the 1950s and 1960s were produced in spring and fall editions. The shape number, description, size, and price of each were listed on the page with pictures of the art ware. Colors were added or dropped from the spring to fall editions. Not all colors were always available for a certain pottery shape in each catalog. Each piece, at some time, was produced in many different finish colors.

As in the 1950s, the art ware continued to have the bright contemporary look of the times, along with some of the plainer more distinguished looking pottery. During this period Red Wing continued producing their line of novelty planters. They continued with the unusual items of the 1950s, such as the piano, banjo, and violin. They also continued with the line of small planters which included a dachshund, donkey, owl, and giraffe.

Once you learn to recognize the look of the 1950s, you will also know the theme of the 1960s. But you will always need to look at the bottom markings to identify the item as Red Wing.

Floraline

The Red Wing Floraline consisted of vases, bowls, compotes, candleholders, and planters produced in various finish colors. Many of them were also finished in two-tone colors. A list of some of the various colors of each era can be found in the back of the book.

Vase. #1633 — 7", semi-matte cypress green, prism type, $38.00 – 48.00.

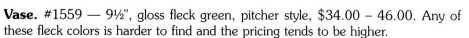

Vase. #1559 — 9½", gloss fleck green, pitcher style, $34.00 – 46.00. Any of these fleck colors is harder to find and the pricing tends to be higher.

Vase. #1580 — 5", semi-matte black, pitcher style, $42.00 – 58.00. An unusual vase and not often found, the price will be higher. As you have probably noticed, the pricing of a piece of art ware depends on many factors. The more unusual items are generally more expensive. From the collection of Bev & Duane Brown.

Vase. #416 — 12", semi-matte cinnamon/light green, gladiolus style, $62.00 – 75.00. Designed to hold gladiolas, this vase was produced in two sizes, both with the same shape number. As you can see, it would make a beautiful bouquet with the flower fanned across the vase. Below you will see the smaller size. Advertised in the spring 1961 Red Wing catalog, this vase sold for $5.50.

Vase. #416 — 12", semi-matte coral/colonial buff, gladiolus style, $62.00 – 75.00.

Vase. #416 — 10", semi-matte cinnamon, gladiolus style, $50.00 – 60.00. Advertised in the 1964 Red Wing gift catalog, this vase sold for $4.50. Both sizes were available in cypress green, matte white, cinnamon, and black.

The following fan vases show the wide variety of color finishes that were used on a single shape of art ware. These fan vases would also make a lovely collection, as they can be found fairly easy in an array of colors.

Vase. #892 — 7½", semi-matte metallic brown/Tahitian gold, $42.00 – 52.00. From the collection of Bev & Duane Brown.

Vase. #892 — 7½", semi-matte blue/white, $36.00 – 48.00. From the collection of Bev & Duane Brown.

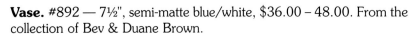

Vase. #892 — 7½", gloss maroon/blue, $52.00 – 62.00. A piece of art ware finished in the maroon color commands higher prices. From the collection of Bev & Duane Brown.

Vase. #892 — 7½", gloss cypress green/coral, Red Wing label, $38.00 – 46.00. Notice the different style of wing label on this vase.

Vase. #892 — 7½", gloss zephyr pink fleck, silver wing label, $44.00 – 52.00. The flower arrangements in these fan vases would have looked similar to ones in the gladiola vase.

Vase. #1235 — 9¾", semi-matte white/green, spiral style, $38.00 – 46.00. This was quite an attractive piece of pottery, and the white color would have fit into any decor.

Vase. #505 — 7½", semi-matte ivory/green, cloverleaf shape, $32.00 – 45.00. This shape was produced since the 1930s and placed in the Floraline of the 1960s.

Vase. #1559 — 9½", gloss zephyr pink fleck, pitcher style, $38.00 – 48.00. The zephyr pink fleck pieces command some of the higher prices of the 1950s and 1960s art pottery, possibly because of popularity and perhaps scarcity.

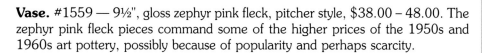

Vase. #1512 — 7", semi-matte cypress green/yellow, long handled bud vase, $44.00 – 60.00. The bud vases would make a very nice color collection and also would be good if you have limited space to display.

Vase. #1510 — 7", semi-matte ivory, long handled bud vase, $38.00 – 54.00.

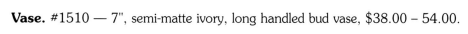

Vase. #510 — 7½", semi-matte green, silver wing label, slender bud vase, $42.00 – 60.00. Notice how the wing label has lost most of its color from use.

Vase. #1621 — 8", gloss cocoa brown/yellow, silver wing label, square bud vase, $48.00 – 65.00.

Vase. #M1510 — 7", semi-matte coral/tan, long handled bud vase, $44.00 – 60.00.

Bowl. #1620 — 10", semi-matte ivory, silver wing label, scallop-edged bowl. $40.00 – 50.00. The wing label on this bowl is in almost perfect condition, indicating that the bowl did not have much use. This bowl is also part of a console set with matching candleholders, shown on page 68 in salmon.

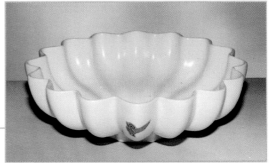

Bowl. #M1572 — 10" x 7", gloss zephyr pink fleck, novelty bowl with handle, $32.00 – 40.00.

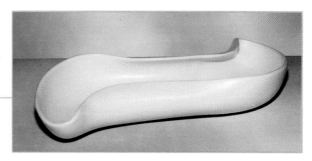

Bowl. #M1447 — 12" x 5", semi-matte white, contoured bowl, $30.00 – 38.00. The contour design of this bowl is similar to Red Wing's Garden Club bowls.

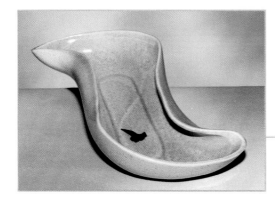

Bowl. #M1447 — 12" x 5", gloss zephyr pink fleck, gold wing label, contoured bowl, $38.00 – 48.00. Notice the unusual placement of the wing label on the inside of the bowl. Except for color, this bowl is identical to the previous bowl.

Bowl. #M5010 — 8", gloss orchid fleck, round footed bowl, $34.00 – 40.00. This is a very unusual color, and it is hard to imagine in what setting this bowl would have been used. Not much of this fleck color is found.

Bowl. #M1492 — 10", gloss fleck green, round low footed bowl, $38.00 – 46.00. Again, an odd color and one not often seen.

Compote. #M1597 — 7", semi-matte ivory, medium pedestal compote, $32.00 – 40.00.

Compote. #M5006 — 11", semi-matte white, contemporary low oval compote, $30.00 – 38.00.

Compote. #635 — 11½" x 7", gloss cinnamon, cornucopia footed compote, $38.00 – 48.00. An interesting piece of pottery, this cornucopia has quite a bit of detail on the outside.

Compote. #M5005 — 10" x 6½", semi-matte cocoa brown, tall oval compote, $32.00 – 40.00.

Compote. #M5008 — 6", semi-matte black, round compote, $42.00 – 54.00. From the collection of Bev & Duane Brown.

Compote. #761 — 6", semi-matte coral/yellow, cherub compote, $85.00 – 100.00. Very hard to find, these compotes are quite expensive. From the collection of Bev & Duane Brown.

Compote. #761 — 6", semi-matte cypress green/yellow, cherub compote, $85.00 – 100.00. There are candleholders that match this compote. They look like the bottom of the compote with the cherubs on them. These candleholders are very scarce and would no doubt be expensive if found.

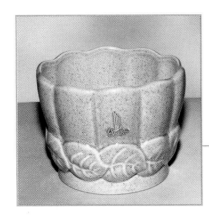

Planter. #B1403 — 5", gloss zephyr pink fleck, gold wing label, violet planter, $38.00 – 46.00. These violet planters originally came with a common red clay insert to plant the flowers in. This was not a common practice with the Red Wing planters.

Planter. #B1403 — 5", gloss gray, violet planter, $30.00 – 38.00. Same shape as the previous planter, different color.

Planter. #B1403 — 5", semi-matte black, violet planter, $42.00 – 54.00. These planters were produced in a variety of colors.

Planter. #1402 — 7½" x 3⅓", gloss lemon yellow/gray, gold wing label, rectangular planter, $38.00 – 46.00. Notice that the wing label is one of the 75th anniversary labels, dated 1878 – 1953.

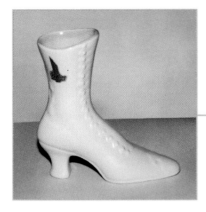

Planter. #651 — 6", semi-matte ivory/green, silver wing label, shoe planter, $80.00 – 110.00. Quite hard to find, any of these novelty planters commands a high price.

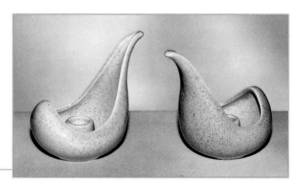

Candleholders. #B1409 — 5", gloss fleck zephyr pink, teardrop candleholders, $28.00 – 40.00/pair. Although the same number and color, notice that one is a darker pink, so these candleholders were not originally a pair. As mentioned earlier, the colors varied with each production run.

Console Set. #M1572 — 10" x 7" bowl, #B1409 — 5" candleholders, zephyr pink fleck, console set, $60.00 – 70.00.

Jardiniere. #M1610 — 10", gloss fleck yellow, scallop top, brass trimmed jardiniere, $52.00 – 68.00. This jardiniere was produced in five sizes, 3", 6", 8", 10", and 12". All the sizes were identical and had the same shape number.

Jardiniere. #M1610 — 6", gloss fleck pink, scallop top jardiniere, $28.00 – 35.00. This jardiniere is missing the original brass handles, which reduces the price considerably. It is included to show you the different size and color.

Stereoline

The Red Wing Stereoline consisted of vases, bowls, compotes, candleholders, planters, ashtrays, and jardinieres. Colors of the pottery were the same as Floraline. However, Red Wing continued to add new colors in every shade imaginable. By the mid 1960s there were many more colors than in previous years. Most of the Stereoline items were also available in the Decorator line colors, which were blue, silver green, and burnt orange.

Vase. #1440 — 6", semi-matte bronze green/pea green, tulip vase, $26.00 – 34.00. This was one of the unique colors introduced by Red Wing in the 1960s. The bronze color was placed over the green and refired. As you can see by the top of this vase, the edges were not always completely covered. This is one of the distinctive aspects of antique pottery — the pieces were not always perfect.

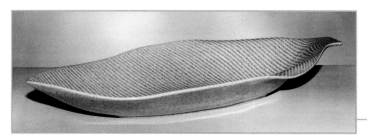

Bowl. #M1453 — 18", gloss fleck zephyr pink, long leaf bowl, $32.00 – 40.00. This bowl was part of a very modern looking console set along with candleholders to match.

Bowl. #670 — 5" x 6", semi-matte hyacinth, hat shape bowl, $36.00 – 45.00. Another unique color done in the same manner as the bronze green. A purple overlay on a blue base created a very pretty glaze.

Bowl. #664 — 14", semi-matte hyacinth, elongated bowl, $34.00 – 40.00. This bowl is part of the Doric ensemble, which includes vases, compotes, candleholders, and this bowl. All the pieces have the same ribbed trim.

Compote. #764 — 13", semi-matte butterscotch, leaf handled compote, $36.00 – 42.00. There were also two urn vases that matched this compote. One of these can be seen at the top of page 94.

Compote. #665 — 11", gloss burnt orange, wide boat compote, $32.00 – 40.00. Also part of the Doric ensemble, this color indeed looks burnt. Notice the black spots in the glaze, especially large on the inside bottom of the bowl. The burnt orange was also used in the Decorator Line.

Compote. #690 — 6" x 9", semi-matte ivory/green, ribbed fluted compote, $38.00 – 48.00. There was a smaller #691 — 7" compote identical to this one.

Candleholders. #661 — 6", gloss bittersweet, tall rimmed candleholders, $32.00 – 38.00 pair. These candleholders would match the bowl shown on page 83 and the orange compote above. The candleholders are also part of the Doric ensemble. The vases look almost identical to the candleholders only taller.

Candleholder. #M1471 — 4¾", gloss fleck zephyr pink, leaf-style candleholders, $30.00 – 40.00 pair. Notice the modern look of these pieces.

Candleholder. #678 — 6", gloss hyacinth, tapered candleholder, $28.00 – 34.00 pair.

Console Set. Bowl #664 — 14", candleholder #678 — 6", semi-matte hyacinth, console set, $58.00 – 70.00 with a pair of candleholders. Although this candleholder is not part of the Doric ensemble but since it is the same color, it looks fine with the bowl as a set. You will find that because of the many items produced in one finish color, it is easy to mix and match for sets.

Console Set. #M1453 — 18" bowl, #M1471 — 4¾" candleholders, gloss fleck zephyr pink, console set, $58.00 – 70.00. You do not often find items as a set. However, it can be fun to purchase one piece from a set and then look for the matching piece or pieces.

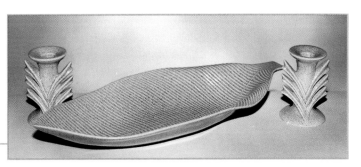

Planter. #1582 — 10", semi-matte bronze green, oval planter, $30.00 – 36.00.

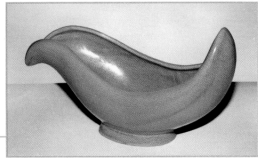

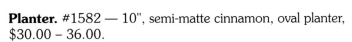

Planter. #1582 — 10", semi-matte cinnamon, oval planter, $30.00 – 36.00.

Textura Line

The Textura line was produced in various shaped vases, bowls, and planters. There were also a bird figurine and candle-holders, called candlesticks in the spring 1963 Red Wing catalog. Like the other Red Wing art ware, Textura was produced in many different color combinations.

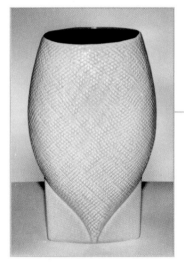

Vase. #B2105 — 10", gloss tan fleck/dark green, footed vase, $38.00 – 46.00.

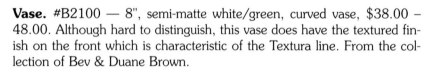

Vase. #B2100 — 8", semi-matte white/green, curved vase, $38.00 – 48.00. Although hard to distinguish, this vase does have the textured finish on the front which is characteristic of the Textura line. From the collection of Bev & Duane Brown.

Bowl. #B2108 — 11¼", gloss gray/coral, teardrop bowl, $32.00 – 42.00.

Bowl. #B2109 — 12¼", gloss gray/coral, rectangular bowl, $32.00 – 42.00.

Bowl. #B2110 — 14½", gloss gray/pink, console bowl, $34.00 – 44.00. The lines on this bowl are raised, forming the texture glaze. It would seem that Textura was designed by Belle Kogan, since all the numbers are preceded by a B.

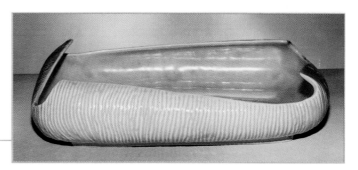

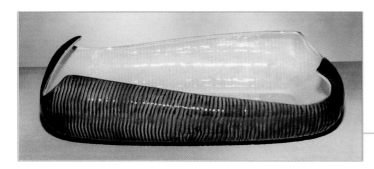

Bowl. #B2110 — 14½", gloss forest green/lemon yellow, console bowl, $36.00 – 48.00. Identical to its gray counterpart, the forest green and yellow combination was quite striking.

Candleholders. #B2111 — 5" x 5", gloss gray/pink, square candleholders, $28.00 – 34.00 pair. Called candlesticks, these were sold separately in the Red Wing catalog like most of the 1950s and 1960s candleholders.

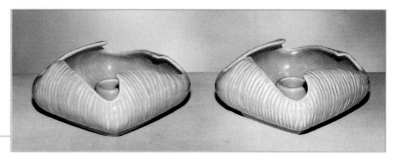

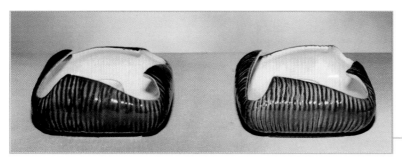

Candleholders. #B2111 — 5" x 5", gloss forest green/lemon yellow, square candleholders, $30.00 – 38.00 pair. Identical to the gray set, they also were used as part of a console set.

Figurine. 10", gloss forest green, perched bird figure, $68.00 – 80.00. Used as a centerpiece in the bowls, this bird has the same texture on the wings and tail as the outside of the bowl and candleholders. As with all the Red Wing figurines, the price reflects the scarcity of this piece and would increase accordingly any console set containing the figurine.

Console Set. #B2110 — 14½" bowl, B2111 — 5" x 5" candleholders, gloss gray/pink, Textura console set, $50.00 – 60.00. These console sets would have taken quite a large space to display.

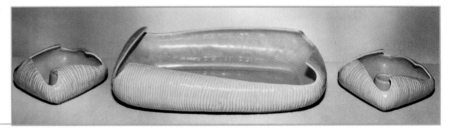

Console Set. #B2110 — 14½" bowl, #B2111 5" x 5" candle-holders, 10" bird figurine, gloss forest green/lemon yellow, Textura console set, $120.00 – 160.00 with bird figurine. Notice how the bird centerpiece gives the console set an added dimension. With flowers in the bowl and candles, the effect would be very attractive.

Planter. #B2101 — 8", gloss gray/coral, rectangular planter, $32.00 – 40.00.

Prismatique Line

    The Prismatique Line was very modern and eye-catching, all pieces having distinguished geometrical prism shapes and being glazed with bright colors. The line consisted of vases, bowls, compotes, and planters. Some were rounded and others had angles.

    Advertised in the 1964 Red Wing gift catalog as smartly styled pieces of Art Pottery with a color treatment that is both beautiful and unique. You will find some of the colors on the color chart beginning on page 149.

    Prismatique art ware is becoming very popular, not only with Red Wing collectors, but also with those who collect Art Deco pottery. Therefore, the prices have been on the rise for the past several years. This line is not easily found in some locations.

    The following items show some of the color combinations, and the two styles of Prismatique.

Vase. #798 — 8", gloss celadon/mandarin orange, medium vase, $60.00 – 74.00. Belle Kogan designed this line. From the collection of Bev & Duane Brown.

Vase. #797 — 11", gloss Persian blue/white, tall vase, $68.00 – 82.00. This is an example of the straight angle style. From the collection of Bev and Duane Brown.

Bowl. #791 — 6½", gloss white/mandarin orange, small bowl, $38.00 – 46.00.

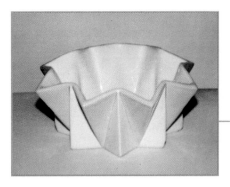

Bowl. #791 — 6½", gloss Persian blue/white, small bowl, $38.00 – 46.00.

Compote. #788 — 5½", semi-matte mandarin orange/celadon, low footed compote, $56.00 – 68.00. In a 1964 gift catalog, Red Wing sold the Prismatique vases in one color combination, and advertised that the colors on the bowl, planter, and compotes were reversed. Red Wing always kept to a policy of changing colors on the art ware from season to season, and as stated in this catalog, reversing colors on the different shapes. Not all colors were available in different seasons' catalogs.

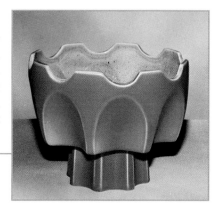

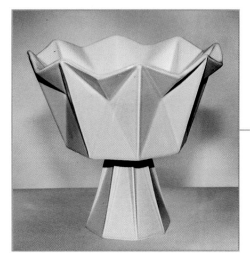

Compote. #796 — 8" x 9½", gloss Persian blue/white, large compote, $72.00 – 85.00. Eye-catching in a Persian blue and almost 5" deep, this was a very large compote.

Compote. #787 — 6" x 6½", gloss lemon yellow/white, straight angle compote, $35.00 – 46.00. Identical except for size to the larger compote, this Prismatique piece was also very attractive.

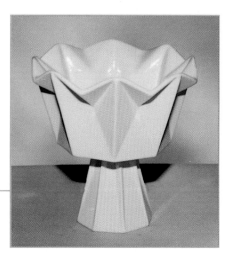

Tropicana Line

Named for its tropical look, the Tropicana Line came in a variety of vases, bowls, and planters. There is also a candelabra and a 13" window box bowl. The art pottery was produced in various two-tone finishes, and all were decorated in one of three embossed styles. These were Desert Flower, Shell Ginger, and Bird of Paradise.

Tropicana art ware is not plentiful but can be found. This line was known to have been sold in the 1963 and 1964 Red Wing catalogs.

The following pictures show one of each of the three decorating styles and some of the color combinations.

Vase. #B2007 — 12", gloss metallic brown/yellow, Shell Ginger vase, $42.00 – 54.00. From the collection of Bev & Duane Brown.

Vase. #B2004 — 10", gloss dark green/yellow, Desert Flower Vase, $38.00 – 46.00.

Vase. #B2005 — 8", gloss yellow/dark green, Shell Ginger vase, $36.00 – 46.00. The B preceding the shape number on all of the Tropicana items indicates Belle Kogan designed this line.

Vase. #B2001 — 8", gloss gun metal gray/pea green, Shell Ginger vase, $42.00 – 50.00. This gun metal color is hard to find and commands a higher price than the other colors.

Bowl. #B2012 — 13", gloss forest green/lemon yellow, Desert Flower bowl, $34.00 – 40.00. This bowl had a similar style to the Garden Club bowls that are pictured beginning on page 97.

Bowl. #B2014 — 14", gloss metallic brown/yellow, Bird of Paradise bowl, $40.00 – 54.00.

Console Set. Vase #B2005 — 8", candleholders #B2505 — 4½", gloss yellow/dark green console set, $62.00 – 78.00. The candleholders in this set are not Tropicana; they are Deluxe Line, Ivy. This set was put together simply to show you that the Red Wing color finishes throughout the years will mix and match to form whatever type of setting you would like to have.

Planter. #B2017 — 8", gloss forest green/yellow, Shell Ginger Planter, $28.00 – 36.00.

Belle Line

The Belle Line was produced in various shapes of vases, bowls, and compotes. There was also at least one pair of candlesticks, finished in various colors and two different glazes. One was a textured matte glaze which was rough to the touch, the other a smooth gloss glaze. The art ware was ribbed at the bottom with a smooth collar at the top of each piece, giving them a contemporary look. There does not seem to be much of this pottery for sale in many areas.

The following pieces give you a look at the style of this line and an idea of how the Belle Line looks. Other colors are listed in the color chart beginning on page 149.

Vase. #842 — 8", textured matte snow white/orange, footed vase, $36.00 – 45.00. This vase is an example of the textured matte glaze used on the Belle Line, with a traditional matte glaze on the inside.

Bowl. #881 — 8", matte snow white/orange, silver wing label, low oval bowl, $32.00 – 40.00.

Bowl. #881 — 8", matte chocolate with white overlay/gold, low oval bowl, silver wing label, $32.00 – 40.00. These are examples of the textured matte glaze used on the Belle Line. The gloss glaze finish is smooth to the touch.

Compote. #848 — 10", gloss peacock blue/emerald green, medium footed compote, $30.00 – 38.00. This piece has the gloss glaze that was also used on the Belle Line. Notice the unusual color combination designed to fit with the décor colors of the 1960s.

Bronze Line

A very decorative line, the Bronze Line was produced in various ornate vases, compotes, urns, and candleholders. There is a wine pitcher and pitcher vase, along with a pair of teardrop shaped candleholders, and a single totem pole style candleholder for a large diameter candle.

Some of the art ware was a solid bronze color, and others had two-tone colors. The following examples show the two-tone finish. Art ware from this line is not often found.

Vase. #763 — 8", gloss bronze/Tahitian gold, leaf handled urn vase, $56.00 – 70.00. This vase was pictured in a 1965 Red Wing catalog advertised under the Bronze Line, and sold for $5.25 each. The same shape number was listed elsewhere in the catalog under vases. Sold in finish colors cypress green, cocoa brown, blue, and matte white for $3.50 each. Comparison indicates that the Bronze Line was special and quite expensive for the times.

Vase. #947 — 5½", gloss bronze/Tahitian gold, cup style vase, $48.00 – 58.00. The actual color on this art ware is lighter and more of a bronze. It appears darker than it is in these pictures, almost a gun metal color.

Chromoline

The Chromoline was one of the most attractive lines of art ware Red Wing made in the 1950s and 1960s. All the pieces had a smooth modern style, and the color was hand painted on the pottery. The art ware was finished in a gloss glaze and in only two colors.

The colors were a rust and green combination, and a blue and yellow combination. Hand painted on the pottery, they had the appearance of water colors, with a slight running which made the colors look blended together instead of in straight lines.

Produced in the early 1960s, this line included vases, bowls, and compotes. The line also contained 6" candleholders, ashtrays, and two sizes of candy dishes with lids. Hardly ever found, the Chromoline tends to command considerably higher prices than some of the other art ware.

Vase. #637 — 8", gloss blue/yellow combination, footed vase, $72.00 – 90.00. This vase also came in a 10" size. Notice the rings of colors, all hand painted on the vase. The blue on the inside gets lighter down into the vase, as if applied thinner than at the top of the vase. The coloring on this vase is very appealing. As you can see, all the items in this line were very attractive.

Birch Bark Line

This was a very distinctive line, made to resemble pieces of birch wood. Produced in the early 1960s, the line had only four pieces, two planters, and a vase. The vase was 7½" high, the canoe came in three sizes ranging from 10 to 17 inches long, and the planter came in a round 4" high size along with a log-shaped planter that was 11" long.

The finish on the art ware was a semi-matte glaze finished in an ivory and brown wipe. It looked very similar to the earlier ivory and brown wipe items only with a plain cinnamon brown color on the inside. Red Wing called it a Birch Bark finish and it was the only one available in this art ware design. Birch Bark pieces are not often seen and usually are higher priced than most.

Planter. #730 — 11", semi-matte ivory with brown wipe/cinnamon, Birch Bark log planter, $85.00 – 110.00. Notice the realistic detail used to give this planter the look of a real log. All the pieces in this line had the same look as this planter.

The canoe was an unusual piece of pottery. Shaped identically to a real canoe with the same finish shown on the log planter, it is hard to say for what use they were produced, perhaps as a planter. The 17" long canoe sold for $5.00 in the fall of 1961, quite a lot of money for the times. At the present time, the canoe has been known to sell for more than $150.00.

Deluxe Line

Shown in a spring 1963 Red Wing catalog, the Deluxe Line was one of the more ornate groups produced in the 1960s. The line shown in the 1963 catalog consisted of two sets. Each set consisted of a bowl, a pair of candlesticks, and a figurine. One set had a shell theme, the other an ivy theme.

The swan figurine from the ivy set was shown at the 1995 Red Wing convention under rare items. These deluxe sets are very hard to find.

Bowl. #B2504 — 14½", gloss fleck pastel green, ivy bowl, $68.00 – 80.00. The other bowl in this line was a shell shape #B2501 — 13".

Candleholders. #B2505 — 4½", gloss fleck pastel green, ivy candleholders, $42.00 – 54.00 pair. The shell motif candleholders were horizontal shells #B2502 — 4½".

Candleholders. #B2505 — 4½", gloss dark green, ivy candleholders, $42.00 – 54.00 pair.

Figurine. #B2506 — 9", gloss fleck pastel green, swans figurine, $135.00 – 165.00. The figurine for the shell motif consisted of a wave with four stacked dolphins jumping over the wave.

Console Set. Bowl #B2504 — 14½", candleholders #B2505 — 4½", figurine #B2506 — 9", gloss fleck pastel green, Deluxe Line Ivy console set, $265.00 – 330.00. The shell console set is also very attractive. It too is extremely hard to find, and the pricing would be comparable.

Garden Club Bowls

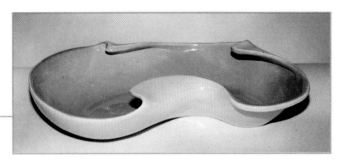

Bowl. #1304 — 13", gloss yellow/gray, contoured bowl, $34.00 – 42.00.

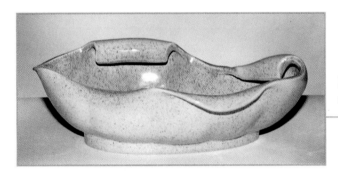

Bowl. #M1463 — 12", gloss fleck Nile blue, curled edge bowl, $38.00 – 48.00.

Bowl. #M1463 — 12", gloss fleck zephyr pink, curled edge bowl, $38.00 – 48.00. The M preceding these shape numbers indicates that Charles Murphy designed these bowls.

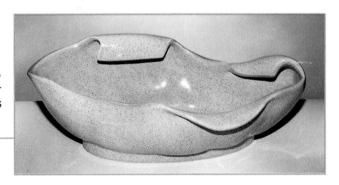

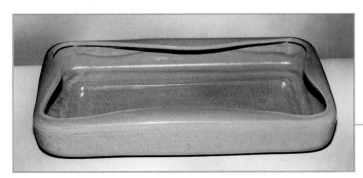

Bowl. #1348 — 12", semi-matte cinnamon, rectangular bowl, $34.00 – 42.00.

Window Box Bowls

Bowl. #407 — 12", gloss orange/tan, bamboo embossed bowl, $32.00 – 40.00. Notice the flat edge of this bowl, formed to set up against a wall or window.

Bowl. #1429 — 10", gloss dark green/yellow, leaf shaped bowl, $32.00 – 40.00.

Bowl. #428 — 14" x 8", gloss pea green/caramel, leaf window box bowl, $28.00 – 34.00. Notice the color on the inside of the bowl, put on lightly so that the green showed through and actually gives the brownish green look of a leaf. The next picture shows the detail on the bottom of the bowl.

Bowl Bottom. Notice the detail on the above leaf bowl. They have hand drawn veins on the bottom. This was done before glazing and firing.

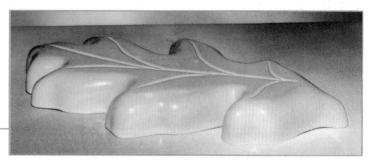

Miscellaneous 1960s

As in previous years, Red Wing grouped many items simply under miscellaneous in their catalog. The groupings were simple labeled vases, or console sets, bowls, and planters. The following pieces of art ware fell into that category in the 1960s Red Wing catalogs.

Vases

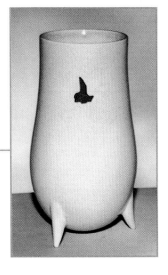

Vase. #M1497 — 10", gloss fleck yellow/ice green, gold wing label, footed bulbous vase, $45.00 – 55.00. Notice the wing label is in perfect condition. Indicating the vase was not used or washed much. Probably designed by Charles Murphy because of the M preceding the number.

Vase. #1359 — 7¾", gloss cocoa brown/sagebrush, coffee cup handled vase, $42.00 – 50.00. Notice the unusual look of this vase, like coffee cups stacked one on top of another.

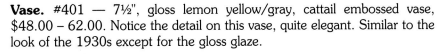

Vase. #401 — 7½", gloss lemon yellow/gray, cattail embossed vase, $48.00 – 62.00. Notice the detail on this vase, quite elegant. Similar to the look of the 1930s except for the gloss glaze.

Vase. #437 — 8", gloss fleck green/colonial buff, contoured vase, $24.00 – 30.00. This vase has a real contemporary look.

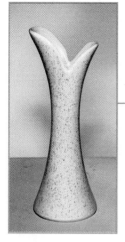

Vase. #434 — 8¼", gloss fleck Nile blue/colonial buff, bud vase, $38.00 – 46.00. You will not find as many bud vases in the art ware.

Vase. #1400 — 8", semi-matte white/green, bamboo motif vase, $36.00 – 46.00.

Vase. #1353 — 7½", semi-matte green/white, fancy leaf handled vase, $40.00 – 52.00.

Vases. #1352 — 7½", gloss blue/yellow, double handled vases, $46.00 – 60.00 each. A pair of these vases were sold as part of a console set with bowl #1347 — 10½". This bowl is shown at the top of page 102.

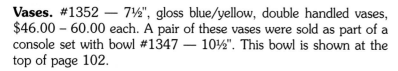

Vase. #687 — 15", semi-matte tan/brown, floor vase, $54.00 – 68.00. This shape was also produced in the 1930s miscellaneous vases and used again in the 1960s Chromoline. From the collection of Bev & Duane Brown.

Vase. #818 — 12", gloss fleck Nile blue, vertical grooved vase, $52.00 – 64.00. Introduced in the spring 1963 Red Wing catalog, this vase was produced in a variety of colors. The colors listed in the spring 1963 catalog were cypress green, cocoa brown, blue, and matte white. From the collection of Bev & Duane Brown.

Vase. #819 — 12", gloss cinnamon, vertical grooved pitcher vase, $58.00 – 72.00. This vase was also introduced in the spring 1963 catalog along with #818 above. Both vases were also listed in the 1964 and 1965 gift catalogs. From the collection of Bev & Duane Brown.

Vase. #B1399 — 5½", gloss yellow/gray, fan style vase, $38.00 – 46.00.

Hanging Vase. #1467 — 10½", gloss fleck Nile blue, silver wing label, hanging vase, $38.00 – 46.00. This vase originally came with a gold chain hooked in a hole at the top for hanging.

Bowls

Bowl. #1347 — 10½", gloss blue/yellow, console bowl, $40.00 – 50.00. This bowl was part of a console set with a pair of #1352 — 7½" vases shown on page 100 at bottom right.

Bowl. #815 — 9", semi-matte white/green, square footed bowl, $38.00 – 46.00.

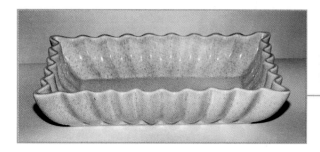

Bowl. #1309 — 12", gloss fleck zephyr pink, ribbed rectangular bowl, $42.00 – 54.00.

Bowl. #M1485 — 8", gloss cinnamon, ribbed triangle-footed bowl, $32.00 – 42.00.

Bowl. #M1603 — 10", gloss fleck yellow, footed rectangular bowl, $32.00 – 38.00.

Bowl. #B1391 — 9", gloss gray/coral, petal-shaped bowl, $34.00 – 42.00.

Bowl. #B1435 — 12", gloss yellow/semi-matte butterscotch, contoured bowl, $30.00 – 38.00.

Bowl. #5019 — 9", semi-matte ivory, rectangular bowl, $30.00 – 38.00.

Bowl. #1381 — 7", semi-matte aqua/ivory, flower rimmed bowl, $32.00 – 40.00. This bowl is part of a large lazy Susan type set using four of #1380 — 9" pieces, which were all shaped to form a circle and trimmed with the same flowers, and this bowl as the center. Each piece was sold separately in a 1964 Red Wing catalog, and they stated that they could be used as an ensemble or as individual pieces. This was a very attractive set.

Bowl. #1370 — 7", gloss lemon yellow/gray, star-shaped bowl, $30.00 – 38.00. This bowl probably also came in a larger size with candleholders to match.

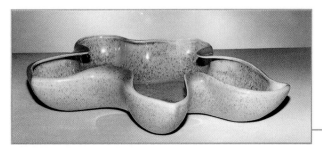

Bowl. #1407 — 12¾", gloss fleck Nile blue, leaf shape bowl, $36.00 – 42.00. This bowl was part of a console set with teardrop candleholders, like the zephyr pink pair pictured on page 82. Nile blue is not a common color to find.

Bowl. #1333 — 13½" x 8", gloss forest green/lemon yellow, rectangular contemporary bowl, $34.00 – 40.00. This bowl was part of a console set with #1384 — 4½" square candleholders to match. It is hard to see the green color on these pieces because they are so low and the edges come out over the base.

Bowl. #1412 — 8", gloss burnt orange/lime green, cloverleaf bowl, $32.00 – 40.00. This bowl was part of a console set with flat teardrop-shaped candleholders to match.

Bowl. #M1486 — 10¾", gloss cinnamon, ribbon bowl, $34.00 – 42.00. Notice the pits where the glaze had bubbled and later cracked off the bowl. Like all antiques, not all pieces of this vintage were perfectly produced.

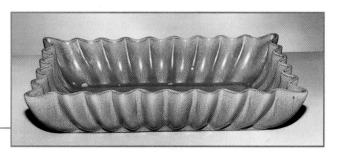

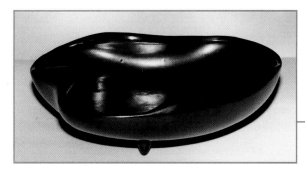

Bowl. #M1491 — 12", semi-matte black, contoured bowl, $38.00 – 45.00. Designed by Charles Murphy, the black color is hard to find and commands higher prices.

Garden Club Bowls

Bowl. #B2015 12", gloss burnt orange/tan, shell shaped Garden Club bowl, $32.00 – 38.00. The Garden Club bowls were designed by Belle Kogan for use by ladies belonging to a garden club and had their own distinct style.

Bowl. #B2013 — 13", gloss pea green/forest green, gondola style Garden Club bowl, $32.00 – 40.00.

Candleholders

Candleholders. #B1410 — 6", gloss yellow, double candleholders, $32.00 – 40.00 pair.

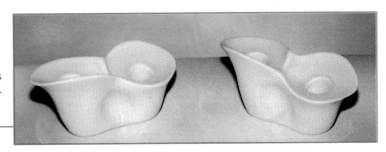

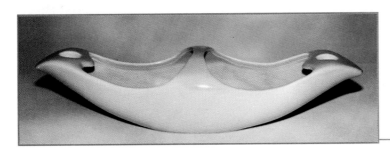

Candleholder. #B1420 — 10", gloss gray/coral, boat shaped double candleholder, $32.00 – 40.00 each. This is a very unique candleholder. As you can see, it was also a bowl that could hold flowers or other decorations. From the collection of Bev & Duane Brown.

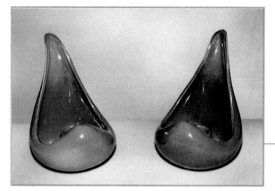

Candleholders. #1409 — 5", gloss cinnamon, teardrop candleholders, $30.00 – 38.00 pair. On the pairs of candleholders, each is bottom marked with the shape number and Red Wing. Some of the Red Wing candleholders you will find are not bottom marked.

Candleholders. #B1412-A — 4½", gloss burnt orange/lime green flat teardrop candleholders, $28.00 – 34.00 pair. These candleholders came with a brass insert in the holes. Notice the number, quite unusual with an "A" following, indicating they are part of a console set shown at top left on page 107.

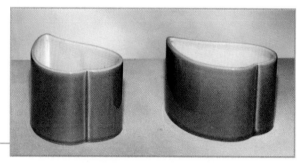

Console Sets

Console sets intact are not easily found. However, you will discover that when you can find them, the price is usually lower than purchasing the pieces separately.

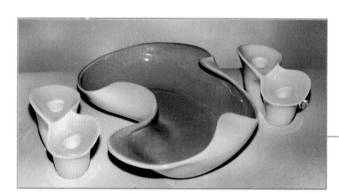

Console Set. #1304 — 13" bowl, #B1410 — 6" candleholders, gloss yellow/gray, console set, $60.00 – 72.00.

Console Set. #1348 — 12" bowl, #1409 — 5" candleholders, gloss cinnamon, console set, $58.00 – 68.00.

Console Set. Bowl #1307 — 10", candleholders #1384 — 4", semi-matte white/green, console set, $68.00 – 78.00. From the collection of Bev & Duane Brown.

Console Set. #B1412 — 8" bowl, #B1412-A — 4½" candleholders, gloss burnt orange/green console set, $44.00 – 52.00.

Planters

Planter. #806 — 6", gloss fleck Nile blue/white, silver wing label, footed planter, $35.00 – 47.00.

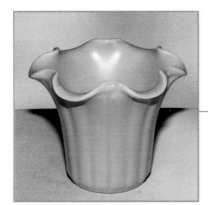

Planter. No number — 4", semi-matte turquoise, violet planter, $28.00 – 35.00.

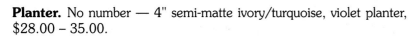

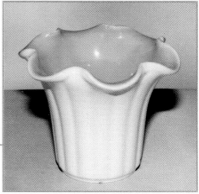

Planter. No number — 4" semi-matte ivory/turquoise, violet planter, $28.00 – 35.00.

Jardinieres

Jardiniere. #110 — 10", semi-matte cypress green/yellow, pedestal jardiniere, $58.00 – 70.00. There were four sizes of these jardinieres; the smallest is pictured below. They also were produced in shape #108 — 8", and #112 — 12". The size is the diameter of the item.

Jardiniere. #104 — 5½", gloss cocoa brown/yellow, pedestal jardiniere, $30.00 – 38.00. Listed in the fall 1962 Red Wing catalog, all the sizes were available in finish colors, cypress green, cocoa brown, blue, black, and matte white.

Ashtrays

Red Wing produced a variety of ashtrays throughout their art pottery history. During the 1930s and 1940s, Red Wing produced several types of ashtrays and what they called ash receivers. One of the ash receivers was shaped like a pelican and looked much like a figurine. The ashtrays were ornate and looked much like small art pottery bowls or shell dishes. There was an ashtray produced in the Magnolia Line and some that were cigarette holders and ashtrays combined. These early pieces are rare and very hard to find.

Starting in the 1950s and 1960s, the ashtrays were produced in many different styles, most looking very traditional. During this period or perhaps sooner, Red Wing produced the famous maroon color wing ashtray, shaped like the Red Wing symbol. It is hard to determine the vintage of the traditional ashtrays, unless they were produced for a special occasion and dated. However, most have the 1950s and 1960s era look.

On pages 111 and 112, you will see the famous Minnesota Twins and wing ashtrays, some of the later ashtrays. You will be able to find some of the later types while you are looking for art pottery. You can also find the wing and Twins ashtrays with some effort.

Common

Ashtray. #M3005 — 11", gloss gold/brown, large square ashtray, $28.00 – 36.00. This ashtray looks identical except for color to one in the Decorator Line, crystalline glazed ashtrays, and has the same shape number.

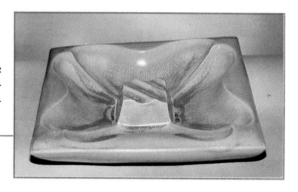

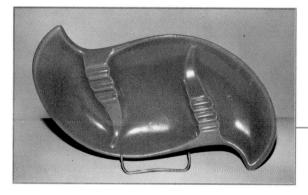

Ashtray. #745 — 6", gloss radiant orange, contoured ashtray, $24.00 – 30.00.

Ashtray. #3002 — 12", gloss silver green, rectangular ashtray, $24.00 – 32.00.

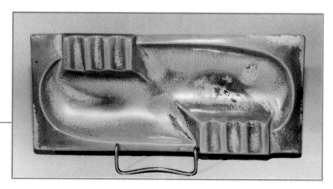

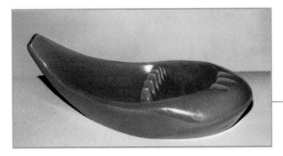

Ashtray. #774 — 6", gloss radiant orange, teardrop shaped ashtray, $22.00 – 28.00.

Ashtray. #746 — 9", gloss bronze green, leaf style ashtray, $22.00 – 30.00.

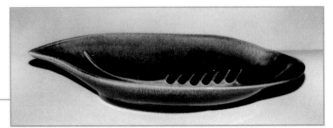

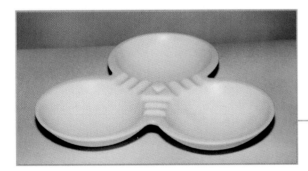

Ashtray. #742 — 9", semi-matte white, circle ashtray, $45.00 – 60.00. Notice the unusual shapes of these ashtrays.

Ashtray. #739 — 5", gloss fleck orchid, leaf ashtray, $20.00 – 28.00.

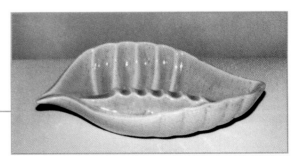

Ashtrays. Right, #828 — 9½", gloss silver green, contoured leaf shape ashtray, $22.00 – 30.00. Left, #741 — 6", gloss caramel gold, contoured heart shape ashtray, $20.00 – 28.00.

Ashtray. #863 — 5½", gloss radiant orange, book ashtray, $20.00 – 28.00. This is one of the unusual styles of ashtray made by Red Wing.

Minnesota Twins

The following two pictures are of the famous Minnesota Twins ashtray. Produced in 1965 for the World Series and shaped like a baseball, this piece of art ware is very detailed. You will not find many of these for sale.

Ashtray. Bottom marked Red Wing Potteries U.S.A., gloss brown/green, Minnesota Twins baseball ashtray, $145.00 – 185.00. Below is the bottom view of the ashtray; notice the detail.

Bottom view.

Wing

The wing ashtray produced by Red Wing was a very popular item. Many other companies purchased it with their advertising logo added. Shaped like the unmistakable red wing that was the pottery's trademark, it also was good advertising for Red Wing. Produced mostly in a heavy red glaze, you may occasionally happen upon another color which would be considered quite a find. These ashtrays are popular with collectors. Associated with the rare advertising and miniature pieces, they are a good find.

Red Wing Ashtray. Top view, red glaze, bottom marked "Red Wing Potteries USA," $48.00 – 65.00. Red Wing also produced this ashtray with their 75th anniversary logo on it. Any of the advertising wing ashtrays will have a higher price. Below is the bottom view.

Bottom view.

Dinnerware

The dinnerware line of Red Wing Pottery was introduced in mid 1930 with the Gypsy Trail Line. Charles Murphy, a designer from Ohio, was hired in 1940 to design dinnerware and art pottery. He created patterns with hand-painted designs for the Provincial Line, introduced in 1941. These patterns were some of the most ornate and beautiful of the dinnerware lines. Eva Zeisel, a designer who had been with Red Wing for some years, created the Town & Country Line in 1946.

Each of the dinnerware lines consisted of a full line of items including casseroles, coffee and water servers, teapots, salt and pepper shakers, and many accessory pieces. The lines were produced in a variety of different patterns and finishes ranging from solid colors to hand-painted flowers, fruits, and other items. There were many different dinnerware lines and patterns produced over the years, some in more limited quantities than others. Patterns ranged from quite simple to quite ornate, requiring many brush strokes.

Some of the early pieces are not marked, but once you are familiar with the look of each pattern, you will be able to recognize them. The later lines were marked usually with a wing stamp and marked Red Wing in some fashion. You will find some of these markings in the bottom markings section beginning on page 145.

Red Wing continued to produce the dinnerware line until the close of the plant in 1967. A huge seller, the dinnerware line created a large place for Red Wing in the history of such ware. Many people collect Red Wing dinnerware. It makes both a beautiful and useful collection, as it can be used for setting a beautiful table or for a lovely display in a china cabinet. You will see from the following pictures that it would be a wonderful collection.

The dinnerware in this chapter, unless otherwise noted, is from the collection of Bev and Duane Brown. They have an extensive collection of all the pottery produced by Red Wing, which includes dinnerware, art pottery, and stoneware.

Gypsy Trail (1935)

Gypsy Trail was the first line of dinnerware introduced by Red Wing in 1935. The line consisted of four patterns which were Plain, Chevron, Reed, and Fondoso. All the patterns were produced in plain colors and included table settings along with many accessory pieces. Most pieces of this line are unmarked.

The following pictures show the Plain and Reed patterns. Due to the age of this line, the patterns are quite hard to find.

Reed Pattern

Produced in orange, yellow, ivory, royal blue, and turquoise, this pattern consisted of place settings, serving pieces, and many accessory items. Among them are pie plates, egg cups, pitchers, covered dishes, and candlesticks.

Reed Pattern Mixing Bowls. Unmarked, 5" – 10" set, gloss orange, yellow, and ivory, $95.00 – 135.00 set.

Plain Pattern

The plain pattern was produced in 1935 in orange, yellow, royal blue, ivory, and turquoise. These were the original colors; several pastel colors were later added. It included a full line of dinnerware along with many accessories, such as several different pitchers, a cookie jar, duck ashtray, and an oil cruet. The pieces could be purchased in a variety of colors per set or a single color.

Plain Pattern Swirl Pitcher. Unmarked — 64 oz., gloss royal blue/white, pitcher $75.00 – 100.00. From the author's collection.

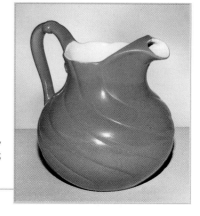

Plain Swirl Pitcher. Orange/white 64 oz., bottom marked Red Wing, swirl pitcher, $38.00 – 50.00. This was one of two pitchers in this pattern; the other was a jug type with ice stop. From the author's collection.

Plain Creamer & Sugar. Turquoise and pink 2", bottom marked Red Wing, $28.00 – 40.00 for both. Notice these pieces are quite small. They almost have the look of miniatures. There was a mustard holder that looked like the sugar bowl with the addition of a lid. You will find that the prices vary per set depending on the color. From the author's collection.

Plain Oil Cruet. Yellow 4", bottom marked Red Wing, oil cruet, $40.00 – 55.00. With the same small swirl as the creamer and sugar, these small pieces made a set along with the mustard holder. From the author's collection.

Plain Salt & Pepper. Turquoise 3", no bottom mark, $22.00 – 30.00 set. Notice that these look like miniature teapots. None of the salt and pepper shakers in the Red Wing dinner lines were marked. You will eventually know them by sight. From the author's collection.

Provincial (1941)

Introduced in 1941, the Provincial dinnerware was the first to be hand decorated. The line consisted of four patterns, Ardennes, Brittany, Normandy, and Orleans. Each pattern has a different hand-painted theme done in beautiful color. You should find that the pieces in this line are marked, with the exception of the salt and pepper shakers and perhaps the candleholders. Most of the salt and peppers produced by Red Wing were not marked, no matter what the vintage. This holds true with a lot of the candleholders also. The candleholders in this line are quite a find, but they are worth looking for because they will add a lot of beauty to your setting.

Brittany Pattern

The Brittany pattern featured a hand-painted yellow rose and a yellow band around the plate. This was the only color finish of the Brittany pattern. The accessory pieces were also hand painted and included serving pieces, salt and pepper, water jug, teapot, and candleholders.

Brittany Pattern Dinner Plate. Bottom marked — 10", hand-painted yellow rose, $18.00 – 22.00 each. As you can see, a table setting in this pattern would be quite lovely.

Orleans Pattern

The Orleans pattern featured a red rose and multi-colored other flowers, all hand-painted. The accessories were also hand decorated and included the same pieces as Brittany.

Orleans Pattern Dinner Plate. Bottom marked — 10", hand-painted red rose, $18.00 – 22.00 each.

Ardennes Pattern

The Ardennes pattern was hand decorated with a leaf border. The early pieces were white with the green leaf band (shown below); later the plates were white with the hand-painted leaf band placed on a light green outer border. The accessory pieces of this pattern were available in two colors, Dubonnet and forest green, and consisted of the same items as the other patterns.

Ardennes Pattern Dinner Plate. Bottom marked — 10", hand-painted green leaves, $24.00 – 28.00 each. This is one of the early plates without the light green outer band.

Provincial Oomph (1943)

Introduced in 1943, the Provincial Oomph line was a heavy utilitarian dinnerware, produced with a combination brown and aqua finish in place settings, serving pieces, and extensive pieces of bakeware. There were no other patterns in this line. Often confused with Village Green since the colors are similar, Oomph has a smooth finish, while Village Green is ribbed on the outside.

Provincial Oomph Dinner Plate. Bottom marked — 10", aqua/brown, $15.00 – 20.00 each. This plate is brown on the back side.

Provincial Oomph Mixing Bowls. Bottom marked — 6", 8" & 10" Bowls, brown/aqua, $65.00 – 80.00 set. Notice that this heavy look resembles the earlier stoneware. From the author's collection.

Provincial Oomph Pitcher. Brown/aqua 60 oz., bottom marked Red Wing USA, $35.00 – 45.00. Notice how this heavy look resembles the earlier stoneware. From the author's collection.

Concord (1947)

The Concord Line was introduced in 1947 and had the most patterns of any of the Red Wing dinnerware lines. There were 19 patterns in all, Blossom Time, Bud, Chrysanthemum, Fantasy, Fruit, Harvest, Iris, Leaf Magic, Lanterns, Lotus, Lexington, Magnolia, Morning Glory Pink, Morning Glory Blue, Nassau, Quartette, Spring Song, Willow Wind, and Zinnia. Too numerous to describe each in detail, some of the patterns featured the design on the accessory pieces, and others had solid colors on the outside. A number of these patterns make up some of the rare and very rare dinnerware items of today. Many of the patterns were hand-painted.

Morning Glory Pattern

Morning Glory was produced in two colors, a pink Morning Glory and a blue Morning Glory. The accessory pieces were finished in green, yellow, and gray. There were not as many accessory pieces in the Concord Line. The following pictures show both colors available in the Morning Glory pattern.

Morning Glory Dinner Plate. Bottom marked — 10½", pink morning glory, $22.00 – 28.00 each.

Morning Glory Dinner Plate. Bottom marked — 10½", blue morning glory, $22.00 – 28.00 each.

Willow Wind Pattern

The Willow Wind pattern was finished with pink and gray leaves on a white background. The accessory pieces match the plates. All similar pieces in Concord Line's patterns have the same shape.

Willow Wind Dinner Plate. Bottom marked — 10½", gray and pink leaves, $26.00 – 30.00 each.

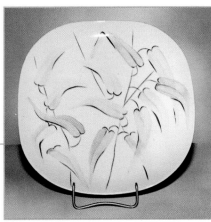

Nassau Pattern

This pattern is decorated with green, brown, and yellow leaves and flowers. Not often found, this is one of the rare Red Wing dinnerware patterns.

Nassau Dinner Plate. Bottom marked — 10½", green, yellow, and brown leaves, rare dinner plate, $80.00 – 100.00 each. This pattern has been known to sell for over $125.00 per plate.

Harvest Pattern

The Harvest Pattern features multi-colored fruit on a white background with a yellow rim. The accessories are decorated the same. This is a very rare pattern and extremely hard to find. Quite attractive, it would make a lovely table setting.

Harvest Dinner Plate. Bottom marked — 10½", multi-colored fruit, very rare dinner plate, $85.00 – 125.00 each. These Harvest plates have sold for over $150.00 each.

Zinnia Pattern

The Zinnia Pattern was decorated with a yellow zinnia and light green lupine leaves on a white background. The accessory pieces were available in gray, copper, yellow, and green.

Zinnia Dinner Plate. Bottom marked — 10½", yellow zinnia, $22.00 – 26.00 each.

Iris Pattern

Iris was produced with multi-colored flowers and leaves on a white background. The accessory pieces came in mulberry.

Iris Place Setting, Sugar Bowl, and Spoon Rest. Bottom marked — 10½", multi-colored, dinner plate, $30.00 – 35.00 each, cup & saucer, $25.00 – 30.00 set, sugar bowl, $25.00 – 30.00 each with lid, spoon rest, $40.00 – 50.00 each. These spoon rests are hard to find, but add a finished touch to a dinnerware collection.

Chrysanthemum Pattern

Introduced in 1947, the Chrysanthemum Pattern was often referred to as Mum. Produced with hand-painted yellow flowers and green leaves on a white background, this was a very pretty pattern. The accessory pieces came in gray or metallic brown. The metallic brown was used as the color for accessories on a lot of the dinnerware patterns. Therefore, some of the pieces were interchangeable. It is sometimes hard to tell which accessory goes with which pattern.

Chrysanthemum Dinner Plate. Yellow flower 10½", bottom marked Red Wing Hand Painted, $18.00 – 24.00. Notice the different shape of the plate, with the edges contoured and rounded up. From the author's collection.

Lotus Pattern

Lotus was introduced in 1952. A full line of dinnerware, Lotus was hand-painted with a flower in a combination of gray, dark brown, and green with highlights of pink on a white background. This pattern had the same color accessories as the magnolia pattern. It was also a very popular pattern.

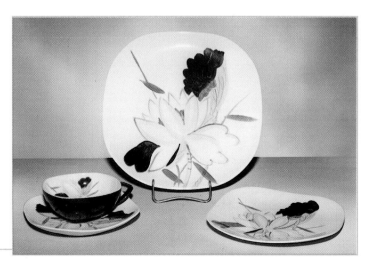

Lotus Place Setting. White and gray flower, bottom marked Red Wing Hand Painted USA, dinner plate 10½", $20.00 – 24.00, salad plate 7", $8.00 – 12.00, cup $6.00 – 8.00, saucer $5.00 – 9.00. From the author's collection.

Blossom Time

Blossom Time was introduced in 1952. A very elegant looking pattern, Blossom Time had a hand-painted flower of pink with green leaves accented with yellow and dark brown on a white background. The accessories came in green and yellow which made the dinnerware even more attractive.

Like all the Red Wing dinnerware, this pattern came in a full line. The plates came in a square shape contoured up at the edges. You have probably noticed by now that the dinnerware plates had many shapes, each adding to the unique look of each individual pattern.

Blossom Time Place Setting. Pink and yellow flower, bottom marked Red Wing Hand Painted, dinner plate 10½", $20.00 – 26.00, cup $6.00 – 8.00, saucer $6.00 – 8.00. Notice the flower painted on the inside of the cup. This is a mark of fine china. From the author's collection.

Magnolia Pattern

The Magnolia pattern was one of the most popular of the Concord Line. It was produced with a hand-painted magnolia flower in a gray and yellow combination with green leaves. It was a full line of dinnerware with accessory pieces in gray, chartreuse, and metallic.

Magnolia Salad Bowl. Yellow and gray magnolia flower, bottom marked Red Wing Potteries, $10.00 – 15.00 each. Notice the touches of black in the color combination. From the author's collection.

Dynasty (1949)

There was only one pattern produced in the Dynasty Line, which was Plum Blossom. Produced in two colors of finish, pink and yellow on a white background. Accompanying a full line of dinnerware, the accessories came in a choice of chartreuse, forest green, and metallic brown.

Plum Blossom Dinner Plate. Bottom marked — 10½", hand-painted, yellow blossoms, $18.00 – 24.00 each. The pink finish is identical to the yellow except for color.

Plum Blossom Place Setting. Bottom marked Red Wing Hand Painted, pink and brown flowers and stems, dinner plate 10½", $18.00 – 24.00, sauce dish $7.00 – 10.00, cup $7.00 – 10.00, saucer $5.00 – 8.00. Notice the forest green on the inside of the cup, one of the accessory colors. From the author's collection.

Village Green (1953)

Introduced in 1953, Village Green was the second most popular of the Red Wing dinnerware. Its sales spanned a decade. This was a complete line including a two-gallon water cooler. Glazed in brown and aqua, Village Green was a heavy utilitarian dinnerware.

Often confused with the earlier Provincial Oomph, both lines were heavy and done in brown and aqua. You will be able to tell the difference due to the fact the colors were put in different places and the Village Green has a ribbed finish.

An identical line Village Brown was introduced in 1955. The only difference was the Village Brown was glazed in a plain brown color. Produced with the same molds, this second pattern had all the same pieces.

The Village Green line can be found quite often. Probably because of their heavy construction, the pieces were not broken as often as some of the other dinnerware. With some searching you could probably find a complete set of this line, unlike some of the other lines and patterns which could take many years to complete a set.

The following pictures are some of the accessory pieces in the Village Green Line.

Village Green Pitcher. Brown and aqua 10-cup, bottom marked Red Wing USA, $32.00 – 46.00. There was also a four-cup pitcher identical to this one. From the author's collection.

Village Green Beverage Server. Brown and aqua 8-cup with lid, bottom marked Red Wing USA, $30.00 – 40.00. This pricing assumes that the lid in not cracked or chipped. From the author's collection.

Village Green Teapot. Brown and aqua 6-cup with lid, bottom marked Red Wing USA, $30.00 – 40.00. Notice the lighter brown and darker aqua colors. This is probably a newer vintage. From the author's collection.

Village Green Beverage Mug, Sugar Bowl, Syrup Jug. Brown and aqua, bottom marked Red Wing USA, mug $18.00 – 25.00, sugar bowl $18.00 – 20.00, syrup jug $12.00 – 18.00. Notice that the chip in the sugar bowl lid has been glazed over. Undoubtedly done in production, you will find this sometimes even on the art pottery. From the author's collection.

Village Green Water Cooler With Stand & Beverage Mugs. Unmarked — 2-gallon water cooler, beverage mugs, gloss brown/aqua, water cooler, $525.00 – 675.00 with stand, mugs, $18.00 – 25.00 each. The water coolers with stands are very hard to find, and the pricing will reflect that.

Anniversary (1953)

Introduced in 1953, this line received its name because that year was Red Wing's 75th anniversary. There were six patterns in this line, Capistrano, Country Garden, Driftwood, Midnight Rose, Pink Spice, and Tweed Tex. Produced in a full line of dinnerware, several colors were available for the accessories. The accessories' colors could be used with the patterns. Many of the accessory pieces in this line had a basketweave texture. Any of these Anniversary patterns would make a lovely collection.

Midnight Rose Pattern

The Midnight Rose pattern was finished with a black and gray rose on a white background. The accessories were available in black. This has a very striking finish, and it is one of the very rare Red Wing dinnerware patterns.

Midnight Rose Dinner Plate. Bottom marked — 10½", gray and black rose, very rare dinner plate, $145.00 – 175.00 each.

Capistrano Pattern

The Capistrano pattern was hand-painted with a yellow-breasted black bird and colored foliage on a white background. The design was sealed under the glaze in order to prevent fading. The accessory pieces were a soft sage green with the basketweave texture.

Capistrano Dinner Plate. Bottom marked — 10½", yellow and black bird, $22.00 – 26.00 each.

Tweed Tex Pattern

The Tweed Tex pattern had no decoration added. It was a plain white color with basketweave texture. Any color accessory could be used with this pattern.

Tweed Tex Dinner Plate. Bottom marked — 10½", white basketweave, $15.00 – 18.00 each.

Country Garden Pattern

Country Garden has flowers and leaves of blue, greens, lavender, and pink on a white background. The accessory pieces were offered in gray basketweave. One of the more decorated patterns, it is quite lovely.

Country Garden Dinner Plate. Bottom marked 10½", multi-colored, $35.00 – 45.00 each.

Driftwood Pattern

The Driftwood pattern was decorated with blue flowers on brown driftwood. The accessories are blue. This is a simple but elegant pattern.

Driftwood Platter. Bottom marked — 15", blue flowered, $36.00 – 40.00 each. Notice the contoured shape of this platter.

Pink Spice Pattern

Pink Spice is hand-painted with flowers in shades of pink and a yellow butterfly. The accessory pieces are lavender and were later produced in pink. This is another very lovely pattern.

Pink Spice Buffet Bowl. Bottom marked — 10½", pink flowered, $46.00 – 54.00 each.

Anniversary Accessories

The following bowls were part of the accessories to the Anniversary Line. All the accessories had this distinguishing basketweave finish. Produced in many colors, the accessories could be used with any of the Anniversary patterns.

Anniversary Salad Bowl. Pink basketweave 10½", bottom marked Red Wing, salad server bowl, $28.00 – 36.00. Notice these pieces' white interior. From the author's collection.

Anniversary Individual Salad Bowl. Pink basketweave 5½" bottom marked Red Wing, $10.00 – 15.00 each. From the author's collection.

Futura (1955)

First produced in 1955, there are 10 patterns in the Futura line, Crazy Rhythm, Colonnes, Frontenac, Golden Viking, Lupine, Montmartre, Northern Lights, Random Harvest, Red Wing Rose, and Tampico. The line had a full line of dinnerware, and the accessories included pitchers, a teapot and cover, a five-compartment nut bowl, and a trivet. The trivets of any line are quite hard to find, but add value to your collection. The Tampico pattern also included a 2-gallon water cooler with stand. Any of the trivets are very rare.

Six of the 10 patterns in the Futura line and the Tampico water cooler with stand are illustrated over the next four pages.

Tampico Pattern

The Tampico pattern is hand-painted in greens and browns with a melon accent on a brown flecked background. The accessories match the dinnerware.

Tampico Place Setting. Bottom marked — 10½" plate, green, brown, and melon, $28.00 – 35.00 each, cup & saucer, $30.00 – 38.00 set. The Tampico pattern is very popular among collectors, and the pricing is considerably higher than the other patterns.

Tampico Water Coolers With Stands. Two-gallon cooler, greens, browns, with melon accent, $525.00 – 700.00 each, with stand. This is a magnificent collection of the Tampico water coolers. Any of the water coolers with stands are very hard to find.

Montmartre Pattern

This pattern is hand-painted in browns and yellow on a white background. The picture gives an international flavor to this pattern. The accessory pieces match the dinnerware pattern.

Montmartre Dinner Plate. Bottom marked — 10½", browns and yellow, $35.00 – 45.00 each.

Golden Viking Pattern

The Golden Viking pattern is hand-painted in a gold and brown leaf pattern which covers the entire plate. The accessory pieces are covered in the same design. A Danish design, this pattern has the look of everyday dinnerware.

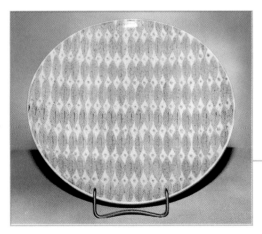

Golden Viking Dinner Plate. Bottom marked — 10½", gold and brown, $18.00 – 22.00 each. The Northern Lights pattern, which is not pictured, is identical to this except it is done in turquoise.

Crazy Rhythm Pattern

The Crazy Rhythm pattern is done is browns and gold on a tan fleck background. The pattern is very modern looking, and the accessories match the dinnerware. This pattern was very popular for everyday use.

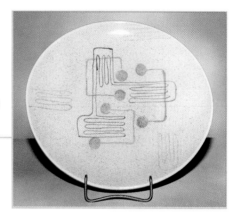

Crazy Rhythm Dinner Plate. Bottom marked — 10½", browns and gold, $18.00 – 22.00 each.

Random Harvest Pattern

This pattern has hand-painted leaves and flowers in rich browns, greens, and copper accented with turquoise and coral on a brown fleck background. The accessory pieces also have the same design.

Random Harvest Place Setting. Bottom marked — 10½" plate, multi-colored, $22.00 – 28.00 each, cup & saucer $15.00 – 18.00 set.

Random Harvest Accessories. Most bottom marked, from center front, clockwise: sugar with cover, $25.00 – 30.00, casserole with cover, $36.00 – 40.00, relish tray $26.00 – 34.00, two-quart water pitcher, $40.00 – 48.00, gravy boat, $25.00 – 30.00, creamer, $22.00 – 26.00.

Red Wing Rose Pattern

The Red Wing Rose pattern was finished with a pink rose with brown leaves on a white background. The accessories matched the dinnerware design.

Red Wing Rose Relish Dish. Bottom marked, pink and brown, $20.00 – 28.00 each.

Casual (1955)

The Casual line was first introduced in 1955 with the Smart Set. There were four other patterns, each introduced after 1955, Bob White, Hearthside, Round Up, and Tip Toe. A complete line, Casual has a wide variety of accessories. There were multiple casseroles with warmer stands, a teapot with warmer as well as beverage servers with stands and a lazy Susan with carrier. Bob White and Round Up also came with two-gallon water coolers with stands. A complete set of any of these patterns would be a magnificent collection.

All of the five patterns in the Casual line are pictured.

Smart Set Pattern

Introduced in 1955, this was a popular set for Red Wing, finished in black, gold, and gray geometric designs on a white background. All the accessories matched the dinnerware.

Smart Set Accessories. Bottom marked, black, gold, and gray design, compartment relish tray, $28.00 – 35.00 each, creamer, $18.00 – 26.00 each.

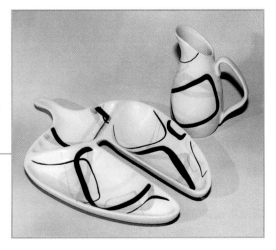

Bob White Pattern

Introduced in 1956, the Bob White pattern was the most popular of the Red Wing dinnerware. Hand-painted in browns and turquoise, the pieces have a bob white bird in foliage on a brown flecked background. The many accessory pieces matched the dinnerware. Other accessory pieces included a pepper mill (which is very rare), a cookie jar, and hors d'oeuvre holder. Many of these pieces are hard to find, but a complete set would be a very valuable collection.

Bob White Place Setting. Brown and turquoise, bottom marked: Red Wing USA, Hand Painted, Ovenproof, Detergent Proof, dinner plate 11", $22.00 – 32.00, cup, $8.00 – 12.00, saucer, $6.00 – 10.00. You will find that most of the dinnerware pieces are sold separately. Occasionally you will find a place setting or cup and saucer sold together. From the author's collection.

Bob White Accessories. Most bottom marked, Bob White design, center front clockwise; bird salt & pepper, $42.00 – 48.00 set, tall salt and pepper, $40.00 – 45.00 set, cookie jar, $125.00 – 175.00 with cover, two-gallon water cooler with stand, $625.00 – 775.00, two-quart casserole with cover and stand, $60.00 – 75.00, hors d'oeuvre holder, $50.00 – 60.00. Bob White is the only pattern that has the hors d'oeuvre holder.

Hearthside

Introduced in 1961, Hearthside was the last of the Casual Line. This dinnerware was produced with brown, orange, and turquoise pictures on a light tan fleck background. The pictures give the image of a fireplace setting with a home and country motif. A full line of dinnerware was produced in this pattern.

Hearthside Relish Tray. Brown, turquoise, and orange, bottom marked: Red Wing, Hand Painted, Ovenproof, USA, $26.00 – 38.00. From the author's collection.

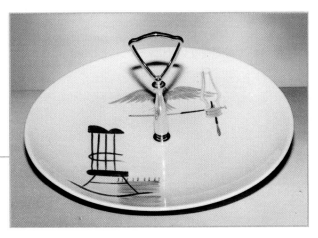

Tip Toe Pattern

Tip Toe was introduced in 1958 and was finished in gold and brown tulips on a white background with a tan border. The accessories matched the dinnerware.

Tip Toe Dinner Plate. Bottom marked — 10½", gold and brown tulips, $10.00 – 15.00.

Round Up Pattern

The Round Up Pattern introduced in 1958 has a multi-colored western motif on a tan fleck background. There are two different western designs of this pattern. The accessories have the same design as the dinnerware. Round Up is very popular among collectors and is very hard to find. You will also notice the pricing is considerably higher than most dinnerware.

Round Up Saucer & Sugar Bowl. Western motif, saucer, $25.00 – 30.00 each, sugar bowl with cover, $52.00 – 65.00 each.

Contemporary (1956)

Introduced in 1956, the Contemporary line included the White & Turquoise pattern and the Spruce pattern. Both were advertised for kitchen, oven, and table.

Spruce Pattern

Finished in blues, white, and brown, the Spruce pattern has the look of dinnerware produced for everyday use. It included the usual table pieces along with casseroles, bean pots, pitchers, a salad bowl, and canister jars.

Spruce Dinner Plate. Bottom marked — 10½", blue and white, $30.00 – 38.00 each. The pricing on this pattern is higher than most of the plainer patterns, perhaps due to scarcity.

White & Turquoise Pattern

The White & Turquoise pattern consisted of the same accessory pieces as the Spruce. It was advertised for kitchen, table, and oven, and it is believed that the table setting pieces were made in limited quantity. Therefore, the place settings are very hard, if not impossible, to find. Finished in turquoise and black on a white background, this pattern definitely has a contemporary look.

White & Turquoise Bean Pot. Two-quart, white & turquoise, bean pot, $42.00 – 48.00 with cover and handle.

Two Step (1960)

Two Step was not advertised as a pattern, rather as a dinnerware itself. Finished in brown and turquoise on a tan flecked background, Two Step was a full line dinnerware. Besides table setting pieces, it included pitchers, platters, and many serving pieces with warmers.

Two Step Dinner Plate, Bowl, Salt & Pepper. Bottom marked, brown & turquoise, dinner plate, 10½" $22.00 – 28.00 each, bowl, $8.00 – 12.00 each, salt & pepper, $18.00 – 25.00 set.

True China (1960)

Introduced in 1960, the True China line was made with china clay instead of the coarser pottery clay Red Wing had used until this point. There are eight patterns in this line: Crocus, Daisy Chain, Granada, Lute Song, Majestic, Mediterrania, Merrileaf, and Vintage. All the patterns were hand painted and carried a one-year warranty against breakage. The patterns included table setting pieces along with serving pieces.

Lute Song Pattern

Lute Song was finished in turquoise and brown instruments on a tan fleck background. The accessory pieces matched the dinnerware.

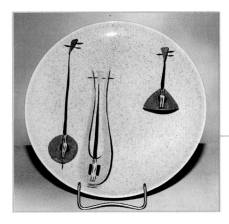

Lute Song Dinner Plate. Bottom marked — 10", brown and turquoise, $25.00 – 30.00 each.

Mediterrania Pattern

Mediterrania is finished in blue and green floral on a white background. Like all of the patterns in this line, the hand-painted designs were soft and very lovely.

Mediterrania Dinner Plate. Bottom marked — 10", blue and green, $28.00 – 32.00 each.

Daisy Chain Pattern

This pattern was finished in gray daisies accented with rust, brown, chartreuse, and green. In all the patterns, the hand-painted finish was sealed beneath the glaze, which kept it from fading.

Daisy Chain Dinner Plate. Bottom marked — 10", multi-color daisy chain, $30.00 – 38.00 each.

Merrileaf Pattern
The Merrileaf pattern is finished in aqua and tan, hand-painted in soft tones. The accessories match the table setting.

Merrileaf Dinner Plate, Cup & Saucer. Bottom marked — 10", aqua and tan, $25.00 – 30.00 each. Cup & saucer, $12.00 – 20.00 set.

Vintage Pattern
The Vintage pattern is hand-painted in soft gray and orchid grapes and leaves on a white background. The design is very pale, as you can see from the picture. The accessories match the table setting.

Vintage Dinner Plate. Bottom marked 10", gray and orchid grape, dinner plate, $24.00 – 30.00 each.

Cylinder (1962)

Introduced in 1962, Cylinder has six patterns: Desert Sun, Flight, Pepe, Pompeii, Tahitian Gold, and Turtle Dove. These patterns were all full lines including serving dishes, casserole, pitcher, teapot, bean pot, and an ashtray. The Flight pattern is one of the rare dinnerware collectibles of today. It is very hard to find and quite expensive.

Desert Sun Pattern
Desert Sun was hand-painted with an orange, gray, and brown sunburst border on a white background. The serving pieces are tan with the orange and brown covers.

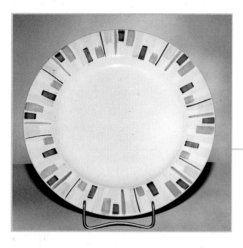

Desert Sun Dinner Plate. Bottom marked — 10", orange, gray, and brown sunburst, $25.00 – 30.00 each.

Turtle Dove Pattern

Turtle Dove is hand-painted with brown and yellow turtle doves on a tan fleck background. The accessory pieces are tan fleck topped in yellow.

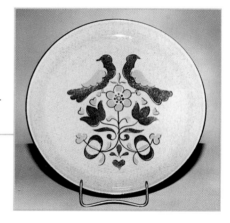

Turtle Dove Dinner Plate. Bottom marked — 10", brown and yellow turtle doves, $15.00 – 20.00 each.

Pepe Pattern

Pepe was finished with an orange and mauve Spanish accent on a tan fleck background. The accessories match the tableware.

Pepe Bread Tray & Bean Pot. Bottom marked, orange and mauve Spanish motif, bread tray, $30.00 – 38.00 each, bean pot with cover, $32.00 – 40.00.

Flight Pattern

The Flight pattern is finished with black, brown, and beige birds in flight on a white background. The accessories are tan with rust and brown covers. This pattern is very popular, and it is also quite rare. You will have to look for quite a while to find any of this pattern, and you can expect to pay high prices.

Flight Place Setting. Bottom marked — 10", birds in flight, rare dinner plate, $100.00 – 135.00 each, rare cup & saucer, $55.00 – 70.00 set.

Flight Divided Vegetable Dish. Bottom marked, birds in flight, rare vegetable dish, $60.00 – 75.00 each.

Pompeii

Pompeii was a full line of dinnerware produced in browns and turquoise. It was quite simple, but elegant.

Pompeii Salad & BB Plates. No bottom mark, browns and turquoise, salad plate, $6.00 – 10.00, bread & butter plate, $5.00 – 8.00. From the author's collection.

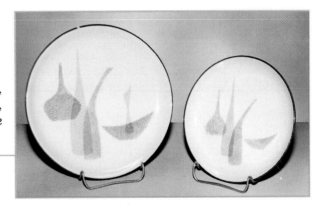

Provincial (1963)

The Provincial Line was first introduced during World War II as a bakeware line. It was reintroduced in 1963 with the addition of the tableware. The tableware is finished in a bittersweet red glaze. The accessories have a tan stone-like finish with bittersweet red glaze on the inside and the lids. They include a bean pot and casserole in several sizes, and two of the sizes are shown.

Provincial Place Setting. Bottom marked — 10", bittersweet red, dinner plate, $12.00 – 18.00 each, cup & saucer, $8.00 – 12.00 set.

Provincial Bean Pot. Tan stone/bittersweet red, 5-quart, bottom marked Red Wing, $34.00 – 42.00 with lid. This pot originally came with a bittersweet red lid like the following picture. From the author's collection.

Provincial Bean Pot. Tan stone/bittersweet red, bottom marked Red Wing, $28.00 – 35.00. From the author's collection.

Like True China (1964)

Produced in almost the same shape as its counterpart True China, Like True China differs in that it was made from potters clay rather than china clay. There are four patterns in this line, Blue Shadows, Brocade, Damask, and Kashmir. A full line of dinnerware, it includes table-setting pieces along with accessories such as a bread tray, teapot, beverage server, and an ashtray.

Kashmir Pattern
Kashmir has a brown design on a rust background. This pattern has a different design than the other three.

Kashmir Dinner Plate. Bottom marked — 10½", brown design, $18.00 – 25.00 each.

Brocade Pattern

The Brocade pattern has a gold design on a blue background. This design is reprinted on both Blue Shadows and Damask. Blue Shadows is blue on a light blue background and Damask is brown on a light brown background.

Brocade Damask Dinner Plate. Bottom marked — 10½", gold design, $20.00 – 28.00 each.

Ebb Tide (1965)

Ebb Tide was less ornate than most of the Red Wing dinnerware. It was finished with a dark green swirl on a green background. There are not as many accessories as some of the other dinnerware lines. They were finished the same and included serving dishes such as platters, salad bowl, and casserole.

Ebb Tide Place Setting. Bottom marked — 10", green swirl, dinner plate, $18.00 – 24.00 each, cup & saucer, $10.00 – 15.00 set.

Ceramastone (1967)

Ceramastone was one of the last dinnerware lines that Red Wing produced before the plant closed in 1967. The dinnerware was made from stoneware clay and included six patterns: Adobestone, Charstone Bleu, Greenwichstone, Heatherstone, Hearthstone Orange, and Hearthstone Beige. The accessories matched and included casseroles, a teapot, canisters, and candleholders.

137

Greenwichstone

Greenwichstone Plates & Sauce Dish. Slate green and yellow fleck, bottom marked: Red Wing, Hand Painted, Ovenproof, USA, dinner plate 10", $12.00 – 18.00, bread & butter plate, $5.00 – 8.00, sauce dish, $5.00 – 8.00. Notice the brighter yellow fleck on the bottom of the pieces. From the author's collection.

Hearthstone Orange

Hearthstone Plate & Sauce Dish. Orange fleck, bottom marked Red Wing, dinner plate 10", $12.00 – 18.00, sauce dish, $4.00 – 8.00. The Hearthstone was also produced in a beige color and was originally made for sale through Sears stores. From the author's collection.

Hearthstone Dinner Plate. Bottom marked "Red Wing" — 10", $12.00 – 18.00.

Hearthstone Orange Single Candleholder. No bottom mark, orange, $55.00 – 70.00 each. A large candle is placed on the flat top. The candleholders from any of the dinnerware lines are hard to find and are higher priced. You will find that any of the Red Wing novelty items are expensive when you can find them. From the author's collection.

Dinnerware Ashtrays

Below are three ashtrays from the Red Wing dinnerware lines. The duck ashtrays are from the Gypsy Trail, plain pattern. The other one is from the True China line and was the same in the Like True China line. Ashtrays from the dinnerware lines are very hard to find and quite high in price. However, if you persist and are able to find the one that matches your pattern, the search is worthwhile.

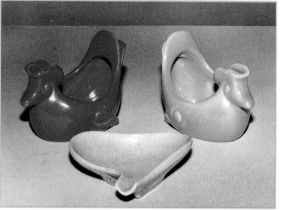

Dinnerware Ashtrays. No bottom marks, orange and aqua duck ashtrays, $30.00 – 45.00 each, tan fleck ashtray, $22.00 – 30.00 each.

Salt & Pepper Shakers

The following pictures are a look at some of the many salt and pepper shakers that came with the dinnerware patterns. These have been grouped together, and they will give you a good idea of what to look for. It is not easy to find a certain pattern, but it can be done. Most of the salt and pepper shakers are not marked but can be identified by the finish design.

Dinnerware Salt & Pepper Shakers. No bottom marks, all are priced per set, outside circle clockwise from center front; Bob White Birds $40.00 – 50.00, Tampico $20.00 – 25.00, Brocade $18.00 – 22.00, Merrileaf $18.00 – 22.00, Lute Song $20.00 – 25.00, Random Harvest $20.00 – 25.00, Anniversary $18.00 – 22.00, center clockwise; Golden Viking $15.00 – 20.00, Pepe $15.00 – 20.00, Cylinder miscellaneous $10.00 – 15.00. This last set was meant to sell with a tall and short shaker like the Pepe. However, some people chose to purchase the two short pieces. They probably liked the look better.

Dinnerware Salt & Pepper Shakers. No bottom marks, all are priced per set, center front clockwise; Two Step $20.00 – 25.00, Spruce $38.00 – 45.00, Bob White tall $40.00 – 45.00, Smart Set 40.00 – 45.00; center, Village Green $30.00 – 35.00.

Dinnerware Salt & Pepper Shakers. No bottom marks, all are priced per set, front left to right: Iris $20.00 – 25.00, Blossom Time $20.00 – 25.00, Zinnia $20.00 – 25.00, Provincial Oomph $18.00 – 22.00, Gypsy Trail Plain $20.00 – 25.00, Brittany $20.00 – 25.00.

Miscellaneous

The following pictures are of miscellaneous items produced by Red Wing that would fit into the dinnerware category.

Salad Sets

Produced in the 1940s these sets consisted of a 13" bowl and four 8½" plates. Hand-painted, each plate was decorated with a different fruit. The fruits are pear, cherries, an apple, or grapes. The bowl was decorated with one of each fruit. The sets are usually found piece by piece and are not often seen. If a complete set was found, it would be quite rare and very expensive.

Salad Set Plate. Yellow pear 8", bottom marked Red Wing Pottery Hand Painted, $38.00 – 46.00 each. From the author's collection.

Miscellaneous Pitcher. Turquoise, unusual bottom marking reads "Red Wing Potteries Inc. Design Pat. Pending," $38.00 – 50.00. From the author's collection.

Juicer. #256, yellow, $140.00 – 165.00. This juicer also has a small glass to fit under the spout. Although rarely found, it would increase the pricing quite a lot to have the set. This price is for juicer only.

Hamm's Mug. Brown, Hamm's beer mug, $60.00 – 80.00 each. Print on mug reads Hamm's Krug Klub.

Cake Carrier. Bottom marked "One Of A Kind", dark green, embossed cake carrier, $150.00 – 225.00 complete as shown. This is an unusual item. It is said that this cake carrier was made for a person connected with Red Wing dinnerware. It is very hard to price one of a kind pieces; the pricing could vary considerably.

Marmalade Dish. Bottom marked — 4½", aqua, pear shaped marmalade dish, $15.00 – 20.00 each. These dishes also came in a larger size with a lid.

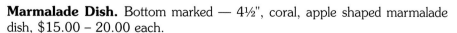

Marmalade Dish. Bottom marked — 4½", coral, apple shaped marmalade dish, $15.00 – 20.00 each.

Novelty Boat Dishes. No bottom marks, light brown, shrimp boat, $12.00 – 18.00 each, butter boat, $10.00 – 15.00 each. It is said there is another larger boat to this set, labeled "Dream Boat."

Teapots. #257 & #260, Bottom marked, Red Wing teapots, #257 — yellow chicken, $115.00 – 130.00 each; #260 — pink lady, $120.00 – 135.00 each.

Cookie Jars

Red Wing produced several varieties of cookie jars over the years. Some matched dinnerware sets and others were novelty creations. Following is a sampling of these jars. Earlier in the chapter with the Bob White grouping you saw an example of the jars made to match the dinnerware. Not all the cookie jars are bottom marked, some have the dinnerware stamp and others no marking at all. You will eventually be able to tell that the unmarked jars are Red Wing by the style. Pricing on these jars assumes that they are in very good condition.

Red Wing Cookie Jar. Bottom marked, yellow and brown, Friar Tuck cookie jar, $155.00 – 185.00.

Red Wing Cookie Jar. No bottom marks, multi-colored peasants, $85.00 – 110.00. From the author's collection. Large serving bowls to match this cookie jar were also made.

Red Wing Cookie Jar. Yellow with brown accents, chef cookie jar, unusual double bottom marked, stamped "Red Wing Pottery Hand Painted," also hand inscribed under glaze "Red Wing USA," $75.00 – 120.00 in very good condition. The hand inscription is identical to some of the art pottery markings. From the author's collection.

Red Wing Cookie Jar. Bottom marked, red flowered, saffron, $165.00 – 195.00. Notice this cookie jar has the look of stoneware.

Red Wing Cookie Jar. No bottom mark, tan fleck, happy cookie jar, $175.00 – 225.00. This cookie jar was named "Happy" because of the verse on the front. It reads, "Happy the children, wherever they are, who live in a house, with a full cookie jar.

Red Wing Cookie Jar. No bottom mark, yellow, barrel cookie jar, $85.00 – 115.00.

Trivet

Red Wing produced trivets in many of their dinnerware patterns. They also made some for advertising purposes. The following trivet was a special Minnesota Centennial production marking the 100th Anniversary of Minnesota. This trivet had quite a lot of detail; the bottom marking included a map of the United States with "Red Wing Minnesota" inscribed in a larger scale state of Minnesota.

Other states and companies also purchased the trivets with their advertising on them. You will find these pieces made in many different colors and markings.

Trivet. Top view red, white bottom marked "Red Wing Potteries," Red Wing Minnesota, and a map of Minnesota, $32.00 – 45.00. A very attractive piece done in the heavy red glaze. Bottom view below. From the author's collection.

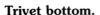

Trivet bottom.

Bottom Markings

Most Red Wing pottery is marked in some manner on the bottom of the piece. There are some exceptions in each category. One example is the candleholders, of which very few have any bottom markings. You will also find some brushed ware pieces with no markings and some of the cookie jars. The reason for this is unclear. Perhaps the pieces were missed or maybe they chose not to mark certain items. However, most of the Red Wing art ware you find will indicate on the bottom that it is indeed Red Wing.

Shape numbers were later added to the bottom markings. These numbers were Red Wing's production numbers. They were also used as the catalog number for an item. These numbers stayed the same on a piece through all its years of production. As mentioned earlier in the book, some of the shapes were produced from the 1930s until 1967 when the plant closed. Letters sometimes preceded the shape number, an indication of the artist who designed that certain piece of art pottery.

The following pictures will give you an overview of some of these bottom markings.

Brushed Ware Markings

The brushed ware line has an ink stamp marking, usually done in blue. You will also find that most of this early line has no colored glaze on the bottom of the piece.

Brushed Ware Bottom Stamp. This is the most common marking you will see on brushed ware.

Brushed Ware Bottom Stamp. You will also find this smaller ink stamp with no circle on the brushed ware. The stamp reads "RED WING ART POTTERY."

Glazed Ware Markings

The early (late 1920s to early 1930s) Glazed Ware was bottom stamped the same as the last ink stamp shown above. This early art ware also was not color glazed on the bottom. It has the rough appearance of the Brushed Ware on the bottom.

Later in the 1930s Red Wing started inscribing by hand RED WING and the shape number on the bottom of the art ware before it was fired. They later also added the inscription U.S.A. to the markings. RumRill line was marked with its line name. Eventually Red Wing stamped these inscriptions on the art ware.

Some of the glazed ware you will find has a letter preceding the shape number. This letter indicated the artist who designed the piece, such as a B for Belle Kogan. An M was added for Charles Murphy.

The following pictures will give you an example of each of these markings, including the RumRill. As mentioned earlier, some of the early glazed ware will have the RED WING ART POTTERY ink stamp that was used on the Brushed Ware.

RumRill Bottom Marking. This bottom marking on a RumRill vase, although hard to see, reads 500 above RUMRILL.

RumRill Bottom Marking. This RumRill vase reads 315 above RumRill.

Early Glazed Ware Bottom Marking. This is an example of the early-incised marking without the U.S.A.

Glazed Ware Bottom Marking Complete. This example shows the marking after the U.S.A. and shape number were added.

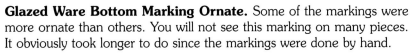

Glazed Ware Bottom Marking Complete. This is another example where the shape number is put before the markings.

Glazed Ware Bottom Marking Ornate. Some of the markings were more ornate than others. You will not see this marking on many pieces. It obviously took longer to do since the markings were done by hand.

Glazed Ware Bottom Marking with Letter. This is an example of adding a letter before the shape number to identify the designer. The letter B was used by Belle Kogan to distinguish her designs. You will see quite a lot of art ware with her mark.

Glazed Ware Bottom Marking with Letter. This example shows the M which was used to distinguish Charles Murphy's designs. You will also see quite a lot of art ware with his mark.

Glazed Ware Bottom Marking with Size. This marking is on the bottom of a planter. Notice that is also includes the size of the piece. You will find very few pieces of art ware with a marking showing the size.

Dinnerware Markings

There is quite a variety of bottom markings on the Red Wing dinnerware. Many include a wing stamp of some sort. One such wing stamp is identical to one of the wing labels added on the outside of some of the glazed ware. Others have a stamp with writing explaining the specifics of the line. For instance the saffron ware is stamped RED WING SAFFRON WARE.

Below are examples of some of the markings you will find on the dinnerware lines.

Dinnerware Bottom Marking. This example shows the written marking including some of the qualities in this line.

Dinnerware Bottom Marking. This is an example of one of the wing stamps used on the dinnerware. If you look carefully, you can see "RED WING" printed in the top of the wing feathers. In the center it states "HAND PAINTED."

Dinnerware Bottom Marking. This is another example of the wing stamps. This one reads Red Wing Pottery with "HAND PAINTED" below the wing. The wing itself is like one of the wing labels added to the art pottery.

Dinnerware Bottom Marking. This small marking reads "RED WING POTTERY HAND PAINTED" with the initials RW inside the circle.

Miscellaneous Dinnerware Bottom Markings. This marking can be found on some of the miscellaneous art ware. This particular marking is on the bottom of a small pitcher.

Miscellaneous Dinnerware Bottom Marking. This marking is on the bottom on a marmalade dish.

Art Pottery Wing Labels

Some of the Red Wing art pottery you find will have a paper wing label glued somewhere on the piece. It is not known what the selection method was for doing this, but articles that are found with the label intact are worth from $5.00 to $15.00 more in value, depending on the item and the condition of the label. The labels were placed randomly on the pieces of pottery. Some were even placed sideways.

The wing labels came in gold or silver with a red wing and red lettering. There is also a smaller, perhaps earlier version that is red with silver markings on it. Some special edition labels have also been found. One such label is like the gold with red wing except it includes writing which marked the 75th anniversary of Red Wing. Following are examples of some of the labels.

Red Wing Label. This is the smaller red label. Probably the first label was used in the 1930s and later changed to the larger silver and gold label. You will not find many pieces of art ware with this label on them.

Silver Wing Label. This is an example of the silver wing label. Notice that it reads "Red Wing Art Pottery." Most of the labels, with the exception of the anniversary label, carry those words.

Gold Wing Label. This is the gold label with identical markings to the silver wing label. The only difference is the color of the label itself.

Anniversary Wing Label. This is one of the special wing labels made in gold and red. Notice the writing marking Red Wing's 75th anniversary.

Color Charts

These are not complete color lists but do provide a good overview of Red Wing production colors.

1920s & 1930s

Brushed Ware
- Dark Green
- Blue Green
- Light Green
- Luster Green
- Bronze Tan

Early Glazed Ware
- Dark Blue
- Light Green
- Green – White Trimmed
- White – Green Trimmed

Medallion Line
- Ivory – Brown Wipe
- Ivory – Green Wipe
- Green – Brown Wipe
- Yellow – Brown Wipe

RumRill
- Pink
- Matte White
- Gypsy Orange
- Aqua
- Eggshell
- Yellow
- Aqua – White Lined
- Ocean Green – Green Lined
- Seafoam Ivory – Nile Green Lined
- Dutch Blue – White Stipple
- Crocus Green Gray – Pink Lined

Other Glazed Ware
- Matte White
- Blue
- Pink
- Green
- Nokomis
- Yellow
- Green – White Lined
- Matte White – Green Lined
- Pink – White Lined
- Coral – Tan Lined

1940s

Glazed Ware
- Blue
- Aqua
- Matte White
- Pink
- Yellow
- Green
- Nokomis
- Matte White — Green Lined
- Pink – White Lined
- Blue – White Lined
- Ivory – Brown Wipe
- Ivory – Green Wipe
- Green – White Lined
- Luster Blue – Coral Lined
- Orange – Gray Lined
- Tan – Green Lined
- Maroon – Gray Lined
- Dutch Blue – White Stipple
- Gray – Yellow Lined
- Luster Blue – Coral Lined
- Orchid – Yellow Lined

1950s & 1960s

Glazed Ware
- Matte White
- Yellow
- Gray
- Cypress Green
- Cinnamon
- Black
- Sagebrush
- Hyacinth
- Orchid
- Coral
- Blue
- Salmon
- Butterscotch
- Bronze Green
- Ice Green
- Walnut Green
- Cocoa Brown

1950s & 1960s, continued...

Luster Blue – Coral Lined
Salmon – Yellow Lined
Coral – Yellow Lined
Blue – Yellow Lined
Lemon Yellow – Gray Lined
Matte White – Green Lined
Coral – Colonial Buff Lined
Walnut Green – Coral Lined
Forest Green – Yellow Lined
Light Gray – Pink Lined
Metallic Brown – Green Lined
Metallic Brown – Butterscotch
Maroon – Gray Lined
Gray – Yellow Lined
Gray – Coral Lined
Cypress Green – Yellow Lined
Cocoa Brown – Yellow Lined

Fleck Colors

Fleck Zephyr Pink
Fleck Nile Blue
Fleck Yellow
Fleck Green
Fleck Nile Blue – Colonial Buff Lined

Decorator Line

Crystalline Glaze
Blue
Silver Blue
Burnt Orange

Prismatique Line

Lemon Yellow – White Lined
Persian Blue – White Lined
Celadon – Mandarin Orange Lined
Mandarin Orange – White Lined
White – Mandarin Orange Lined

Belle Line

Olive Green – Moss Green Lined
Chocolate with White Overlay
Snow White – Orange Lined
Peacock Blue – Emerald Green Lined

Ashtrays

Silver Green
Burnt Orange
Radiant Orange
Metallic Brown
Caramel Gold
Orchid
Matte White

Index

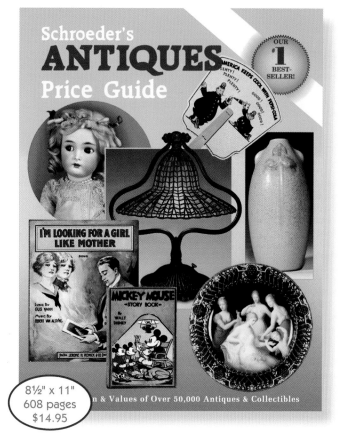